Praise for *A Parent's Guide to the Christian College*

"Every parent who reads this book will have the tools to help maximize their child's time in college. Todd Ream, Tim Herrmann, and Skip Trudeau cover the breath of campus life with fresh research and engaging case studies that provide parents a behind-the-scenes look at the Christian college. Parents not only gain an understanding of what to expect during the college years, but now have specific talking (and listening) points for those upcoming calls, texts, and tweets from their child."

—**Kimberly C. Thornbury**, Vice President for Student Services and Dean of Students, Union University

"Written by three respected and well-known veterans of Christian higher education, this excellent book is indispensable for parents who want the most from their child's Christian college experience. The authors are both practical and empathetic in providing a foundation that explains and values the holistic development of college students. As a parent, you will be encouraged and inspired by the insights that will inform your relationship with your son or daughter. You will also gain valuable advice about interacting with the college he or she attends."

—**Brad Lau**, Vice President for Student Life, George Fox University

"This is much more than a parent's guide to the Christian college. It is a landmark text providing the reader with an in-depth understanding of the potential of the Christian College experience. It offers the tools needed to discern which Christian college, out of the hundreds that exist, promises the best fit for student and family. It is packed full of wisdom on how parents can support and challenge their children as they move through the college years. The credibility of this book rests solidly on the Christian faith and practical experience of its authors as well as their splendid use of current research in higher education. This is a must read for parents, admissions recruiters, faculty, and student development professionals."

—**Barry J. Loy**, Vice President of Student Development and Dean of Students, Gordon College

"Todd, Tim, and Skip have written a remarkable book that will extend your parenting into a full partnership with the Christian college your child is attending. They want you to know that this sacred journey of young adults through the successes, failures, crises, and triumphs of the college experience can ultimately lead to mature and faithful college graduates well positioned to accomplish God's call on their life. This book should be required reading for all parents who want that same outcome."

—**Jon Wallace**, President, Azuza Pacific University

"Todd Ream, Tim Herrmann, and Skip Trudeau are three outstanding colleagues who have not only thought deeply about the potential impact of Christian higher education, but also have hands-on, practical experience watching students develop their minds and spirits during the college years. They are wise leaders, thoughtful scholars, and Christ-centered professionals. Read this book and learn how you can help your students thrive, then get ready to see your sons and daughters transformed. What an amazing journey college is!"

> —**Jane Hideko Higa**, Vice President for Student Life and Dean of Students, Westmont College

"What a thoughtful and needed resource this Parent's Guide *will be for those of us in Christian higher education as we speak with parents about what to expect in their student's Christian college experience! I've been at this for twenty-five years, and reading it was helpful for me to review and affirm what I love about what we do. It is also a great reminder of the parent's role in helping make this a great experience for their student."*

> —**Mark Troyer**, Vice President for Student Development, Asbury College

"Finally, here is a book that brings parents and students to the table concerning the holistic purpose of Christian higher education. A Parent's Guide to the Christian College *will enable parents and students to understand the conversation about the purpose of Christian higher education and become appropriate advocates for that purpose. This is the type of parent and student advocacy I openly welcome."*

> —**Christopher T. Abrams**, Vice President of Student Development, Malone University

"This valuable book provides clarity on how college will impact parent's most sacred 'resource'—their children. It provides a clear window into how students develop at college, particularly at a Christian college. Maybe more importantly, it also gives guidance on how parents can partner with college educators to maximize the experience."

> —**Stephen T. Beers**, Vice President for Student Development, John Brown University

From success in the classroom to finding a spiritual community, the authors comprehensively analyze the domains of college life and offer practical guidance for parents wanting to help their children engage in a college experience that combines excellence in academics with a nurturing Christian community. A Parent's Guide to the Christian College *features a powerful, in-depth discussion of the value of placing common worship at the center of collegiate life. In short, the authors have fashioned a valuable tool for thoughtful Christian parents at a time when Christian higher education seeks to emphasize the integral connection between faith and knowledge."*

> —**Ken Starr**, President, Baylor University & Former Court of Appeals Judge, Solicitor General, and Independent Counsel

A *Parent's Guide* to the
CHRISTIAN
COLLEGE

A Parent's Guide to the
CHRISTIAN
COLLEGE

Supporting Your Child's
Heart, Soul, and Mind
during the College Years

TODD C. REAM, TIMOTHY W. HERRMANN,
& C. SKIP TRUDEAU

Abilene Christian University Press

A PARENT'S GUIDE TO THE CHRISTIAN COLLEGE
Supporting Your Child's Heart, Soul, and Mind during the College Years

ACU
PRESS

Copyright 2011 by Todd C. Ream, Timothy W. Herrmann & C. Skip Trudeau

ISBN 978-0-89112-049-0
LCCN 2011007762

Printed in the United States of America

Scripture quotations, unless otherwise noted, are from The Holy Bible, New International Version. Copyright 1984, International Bible Society. Used by permission of Zondervan Publishers.

LIBRARY OF CONGRESS CATALOGING-IN-PUBLICATION DATA
Ream, Todd C.
 A parent's guide to the Christian college : supporting your child's heart, soul, and mind during the college years / Todd C. Ream, Timothy W. Herrmann & C. Skip Trudeau.
    p. cm.
 Includes bibliographical references and index.
 ISBN 978-0-89112-049-0 (alk. paper)
 1. Christian universities and colleges--United States. 2. College student orientation--United States. 3. Education, Higher--Parent participation--United States. I. Herrmann, Timothy W. II. Trudeau, C. Skip. III. Title.
 LC621.R43 2011
 378'.071--dc22

                                                                    2011007762

Cover design by Jennette Munger
Interior text design by Sandy Armstrong

For information contact:
Abilene Christian University Press
1626 Campus Court
Abilene, Texas 79601

1-877-816-4455 toll free
www.abilenechristianuniversitypress.com

11 12 13 14 15 16 / 7 6 5 4 3 2 1

To
Charles & Linda Ream,
Bob & Ruthe Herrmann, &
Craig & Carole Trudeau

CONTENTS

FOREWORD

by Stanton L. Jones
Provost, Wheaton College

If the glossy viewbooks generated by all the higher education institutions are to be believed, every college and university has beautiful weather, amazing facilities, stellar faculty and students, and is absolutely the best at "training the leaders of tomorrow" and "preparing students for excellence." Sorting through the facts and realities to separate myth from fact can be perplexing.

Parents who are thoughtful Christians confront not only the challenge of discerning the realities behind the marketing materials, but also must strike a balance between the ideals you hold out for the education of your beloved child and the practicalities of your particular situation including your family finances and the spiritual maturity and college-readiness of your student.

But it is important to begin with our ideals. What thoughtful Christian parent would not desire more for their child than just growth in knowledge and skill? Don't we desire also growth in maturity of faith, growth into Christ-likeness, growth into goodness, growth toward becoming the man or woman that you know God desires your child to become?

As Todd C. Ream, Timothy W. Herrmann, and C. Skip Trudeau point out in this excellent volume, some young adults will experience growth in knowledge and skill *and* growth in faith at a secular college or university. Attendance at a Christian college is not a prerequisite for a Christian young person to have a good college experience. As a graduate of two huge, tier-one, national research universities, I experienced this firsthand. For me, Texas A&M and Arizona State University were places of growth both intellectually and spiritually. But it was not until I came to a Christian liberal arts college to serve on the faculty (and later in administration) that I began to experience what I consider to be a close approximation of the ideal of what a college education should be.

As an undergraduate and later as a graduate student, I experienced both intellectual and spiritual growth, but bringing those two together was a great challenge. This was in no small part because, by and large, the contemporary nonreligious college and university has given up on thoughtfully seeking to shape the personal and spiritual growth of students. Todd, Tim, and Skip discuss this reality, reflecting on how most contemporary colleges have abandoned the idea of serving *en loco parentis*, literally in the place of the parents, of taking over part of the responsibility of parenting and shepherding your children.

In large part, this is intentional. To shape not just intellectual and practical skill but also religious faith, character, values, life philosophy, and almost everything that is truly meaningful, universities would have to have some coherent goal at which to aim. But at our "secular" institutions of higher learning, only the value of "tolerance" today serves as a common foundation, an ultimately incoherent foundation. As public intellectual Stanley Fish recently and correctly said, it is impossible for universities to "engage in moral and civic education" because to do so requires "deciding in advance which of the competing views of morality and citizenship is the right one."[1] If educators are by intent and inclination unwilling to make commitments to what is right, to a coherent and consistent vision of morality and citizenship, educators by definition are frozen at the starting line of the shaping of the person. The situation is rather like a race for sprinters in which everyone is encouraged to run off in any direction they desire.

Christian higher education, in contrast, starts with a coherent vision of the Good, the True, and the Beautiful that can serve as a capable guide as we seek to shape the whole person of the student. It is for this reason that the Christian church, since its earliest days, supported a vision of holistic education and has fostered Christian education. As my Wheaton College colleague, philosopher Arthur F. Holmes, discussed in his book *Building the Christian Academy*,[2] the earliest Christian liberal arts academy was established by wise believers in Alexandria, Egypt in the third century, and has existed in various forms ever since as cathedral schools, seminaries, academies, and as the founding ideal for the earliest European universities of Bologna, Paris, Oxford, and Cambridge. The Christian academy was established for four critical reasons: 1) to interact with the best thinking of unbelievers for the sake of evangelism and apologetics; 2) to learn from nonchristian thought for the sake of truth in the church; 3) to worship God by thinking broadly and well; and 4) to provide a holistic education which, recognizing that the mind is interconnected with the heart and soul, that knowledge cannot be separated from character, seeks to emphasize growth in knowledge and in faith. This original vision now largely exists in the form of the contemporary Christian college in America.

This *Parent's Guide* offers abundant wisdom about how thoughtful Christian parents can foster the growth of their son or daughter as they attend a Christian college. The authors present a compelling holistic vision of the development of the college student, and of how loving parents can support that growth. They give concrete tools of insight and information that can help parents avoid stunting their child's growth through negligence or, at the opposite extreme, by functioning as enmeshed "helicopter parents" who blunt the emergence of their student into adulthood by being too intrusively involved and doing too much for their child.

Todd, Tim, and Skip present a wonderful vision of the core of Christian education as centering on worship. Indeed, the true worship of the great Triune God, Father, Son and Holy Spirit, is the cornerstone of Christian life. In addition to the practice of "common worship" that serves as our anchor in college chapel services and church, the Christian college also has the opportunity to foster an entire lifestyle of worship. As an undergraduate and graduate student at nonreligious institutions, I survived and even grew as a Christian, but was blunted in my realization that Christ was Lord over all of life, and that I could worship him in truth with my mind every bit as much as with my spirit and actions. It is this vision of bringing the Lordship of Christ to bear on the life of the mind that animates the project that marks a good number of the Christian colleges, that of striving to "integrate Christian faith and scholarship." Worship is not limited to a religious service, but rightly spills out into all areas of life including the intellectual life, and so Christian higher education is an opportunity for students to learn how to rightly order every facet of life under God's truth and God's sovereignty, and thus learn how to offer up all facets of life in worship of the one true God.[3]

Christian parenting is properly directed at doing everything we parents can to encourage our children to become the men and women that God intends them to be. Sending your child to a Christian college can be a proper extension of that work of grace in your child's life. This book can be a thoughtful guide for your efforts as a parent as you seek to extend God's work in the life of your child through his or her higher education experience.

The way forward is challenging. A Christian college education is not for everyone, and it is not possible for everyone. The price of a private Christian college education can be intimidating in a time of financial challenge, though I encourage you to investigate the possibilities thoroughly, as much more generous financial aid is available than parents often think. Discovering the realities behind the hype of college recruitment and marketing materials is equally a challenge, especially when more than a few schools present their "historic religious affiliation" as more than it really is, namely, a mere historical oddity. But with this book as a guide, you're well on your way to facilitating the growth of your son or daughter.

May God bless and direct your efforts as parents, and may God bless your use of this guidebook.

INTRODUCTION

The beginning of the academic year comes with both great excitement and great challenges. These sentiments prove to be as true for me today as they did during my first years working at a Christian college. As a relatively new, young, and admittedly naïve dean of students, I was trying to make sure that everyone, especially our first-year students, felt at home. Move-in day, orientation week, and the first week of classes had passed. We were beginning to enter into that phase of the academic year when new students often realize that their choice of college came with some relatively long-standing ramifications. Classes were not only getting harder, but the newness of having roommates was subsiding. For a generation of young persons for whom private bedrooms were the rule and not the exception, these unwanted intruders were beginning to pose challenges possibly larger than those posed by their new classes.

Having lived through this wave of roommate conflict the previous academic year, my colleagues and I decided to develop a system of conflict resolution designed to embody the distinct qualities of Christian reconciliation. As educators serving at a Christian college, we concluded that we had an obligation to weave the truths of the biblical narrative into our policies. As a result, we developed a plan to help students work through conflicts with their roommates that involved a set of guided interactions that adhered to biblical teachings and followed a set timeline. In this plan, students would meet with their residence director to identify the nature of the conflict and then set goals to resolve it. They would then meet again with their residence director no sooner than a week later (unless there was an emergency) to review what goals were met and to determine if any further goals were needed. What we were trying to teach our students was how to confront one another constructively and ultimately how to forgive.

This new set of strategies was working relatively well until we encountered a situation involving three roommates. The first roommate was very reserved and unwilling to confront the differences causing conflict between her and her roommates. The other two were more outgoing yet equally disinterested in confrontation. The residence director tried several times to meet with these three young women and discuss the nature of the conflict. All of her efforts were met with the demand for new roommates. She replied that she could not grant that demand unless the three roommates first sat down and tried to work out their differences.

This situation dragged on for two or three days before the parents began calling my office. The parents of the first student told me that their daughter was just too reserved to undergo a confrontation with her roommates and that if I did not overrule the residence director's decision, they would call the college president. Later that same day, the parents of the second student called, asking if I was considering granting the room change their daughter was demanding. They then went on to say how disappointed they would be in me and in the college if I did, explaining that they worked hard to provide their daughter with a Christian education and that learning to live with others was an important lesson. They were going to hold the college and me responsible if we failed to try to teach their daughter that lesson. The parents of the third student never contacted the university.

Looking back on that experience, I see the second set of parents as a positive example I would offer to you. The first set just wanted to solve the problem on behalf of their daughter. However, the second set were not only aware of the details of the situation, but understood the policies and procedures we had designed to teach certain lessons. They loved their daughter but realized that at age eighteen she still had a lot to learn. They called to make sure we did our part to educate her. While I must admit I generally find confrontation unpleasant, there was something reassuring about getting a call from parents who wanted us to ask more, not less, of their daughter. They understood that a valuable learning experience was either about to be capitalized upon or lost. They wanted to be sure it was the former and not the latter. My hope is that this book provides an aid in understanding the Christian college and what you can do to help your child get the most out of this important experience.

Two Considerations

Two driving convictions shape this book. The first conviction is the one I just mentioned: proper forms of parental involvement in the college experience are quite beneficial. However, as I also just mentioned, not all forms of parental involvement are the same. In its January-February 2007 issue, the Duke University alumni magazine ran a cover story entitled "Helicopter Parents."[1] Shortly thereafter, the spring 2007 issue of the Miami University (Ohio) alumni magazine carried a cover story entitled "Helicopter Parents Hover over Campus."[2] Since that time, a host of similar stories have appeared.[3] The sheer volume of such stories confirms what administrators and faculty members on college and university campuses have been seeing for the past decade: the relationship between college students and their parents has undergone a significant change.

Slipping further and further into the past are parents who assumed their daughters and sons were on their own once they entered the campus gates. In contrast, I now see some parents hovering like search and rescue helicopters, prepared to bring comfort and aid at the first signs of distress. I see other parents who hover like attack helicopters, ready to engage in whatever offensive maneuvers are deemed necessary to ensure the protection of their daughters and sons. Regardless of how they make their presence known, most parents are now more present and active in their children's college years than previous generations.

While the phrase "helicopter parents" carries with it a negative connotation, I think that the previous generation of parents was perhaps too removed from the college experience. Parental involvement greatly benefits not only the student but also the school. During their college years, students have a lot of difficult questions to answer, beginning first and foremost with "What is my calling in life?" Answers to questions like this are not easy to come by. But they can be found when college leaders and parents work together to help students discern God's call. The question here is not whether parents should be involved, but in what manner.

This is by no means the first guide to the college experience, but the majority of current guides fail to consider the unique characteristics of Christian colleges. As mentioned earlier, I believe that the Christian college or university has a responsibility to weave the biblical narrative into all aspects of campus life. In order to do this, all campus activities should be oriented toward the calling that God gives us all—to offer praise and worship to him.

My second conviction is thus that the Christian college or university is a place where students should be challenged to recognize that calling and then to discover how they can use their strengths to answer it. Employment is but one of the ways that particular calling is fulfilled. Christian colleges and universities train people to be attorneys, physicians, ministers, and teachers, but these institutions should also provide guidance for how to honor God as a spouse, a parent, a neighbor, and above all others, members of Christ's body—the church. This book will help you understand how we, parents and educators, can work together to support the call God extends to our young people.

A Note about Authorship

Although this book employs a singular, first-person voice, it is actually co-authored by three different people. Together, we represent decades of experience in at least eight different institutions. We have served on the faculty and in student development, serving in every capacity in student development, ranging from entry-level residence directors to chief student development officers. More important than the positions we have held, we have worked side by side with parents during times of great sorrow and great joy. While we do not pretend to have all of the answers, we have been fortunate to be surrounded by people who have helped us learn from both our successes and our mistakes over the years. Our hope is that those lessons will prove instructive for you.

A Note about the Organization of the Book

The book is organized into seven chapters. These seven chapters are divided into two sections. The first section discusses the three domains of Christian college experiences: common worship; the classroom; and out-of-class elements. The second section addresses the seasons of life at a Christian college— stretching from the time a student enters to the time she or he graduates.

Each of the chapters is then broken into three parts. First, each chapter opens by discussing how a particular movie carries misconceptions about the college experience. I have chosen to use these motion pictures because they provide helpful illustrations, some serious, some silly, of particular aspects of college life. I then will recast the college experience from a distinctively Christian perspective. Second, each chapter offers a brief overview of what the current literature says about the subject of the chapter. Finally, each chapter closes by providing parents with practical considerations related to a particular season of life at a Christian college.

PART ONE: The Domains of College Life

Chapter One, "Where Two or Three Are Gathered: The Centrality of Common Worship" Movie: *A Beautiful Mind* (2001)

I open by arguing that common worship of the Triune God is the definitive practice of the Christian college. As a result, it properly orders the relationships its community members share with one another as well as the other practices in which they participate. This chapter will show that, while academics are important, they must be viewed through a spiritual lens. Faith and learning are not separate aspirations here, but are drawn into a common relationship through the combination of intellectual practices and spiritual community. Some of the practical considerations covered in this chapter include chapel attendance, guest speakers, matters of doctrine, the importance of various Christian traditions, and worship styles.

Chapter Two, "Pencils Down, Time's Up: The Nature of the Classroom" Movie: *Mona Lisa Smile* (2003)

As an extension of the experience of common worship, the classroom, the laboratory, and the studio become places where students are challenged and strengthen their understanding of what it means to be human. Such an understanding is not simply intellectual or cognitive but impacts the whole of one's identity. Some of the practical considerations covered in this chapter include academic freedom, academic integrity, academic rigor, elective courses, examinations, faculty/student relations, general education courses, and grades.

Chapter Three, "Not All Fun and Games: College beyond the Classroom" Movie: *Animal House* (1978)

Popular conceptions and misconceptions of college life beyond the classroom include various forms of adolescent frivolity. In contrast, well-designed out-of-class experiences facilitate just as much learning as those within a classroom. A short list includes community service, intramural sports, intercollegiate athletics, leadership opportunities, missions, and social activities. These experiences are not designed to be extra-curricular in nature. Rather, when designed well, they draw faith and learning into an even closer relationship by extending the lessons learned in both common worship and the classroom. Some of the practical considerations covered in this chapter include alcohol and drug use, entertainment (movies, video games, etc.), friendships, sexuality, social networking websites, and spiritual formation groups.

PART TWO: The Seasons of College Life

Chapter Four, "When the Only Thing to Fear Is Fear Itself: Lessons from the First Year" Movie: *Revenge of the Nerds* (1984)

The first year is often the most difficult year in college for students as they leave the comforts of their former social networks and are challenged to establish new relationships and identities. At the same time, students face the challenges of meeting a new set of academic expectations and navigating new bureaucracies. Any one point of transition is difficult, but all three at the same time can be overwhelming. Perhaps in a more intense fashion than at any other time in their lives, students during the first year face the challenge of appreciating themselves as social beings. Thus, some of the practical considerations covered in this chapter include eating, sleeping, study habits, homesickness, physical exercise, and roommate conflict.

Chapter Five, "Prosperity Abounds: Rethinking Success during the College Years"
Movie: *With Honors* (1994)

Too many college students measure success in quantitative terms. From an early age, they are taught to accumulate activities and achievements that translate into lines on their résumés. In this context, decisions like picking a major or a thesis topic come to be viewed as moments which teach students to think about their understanding of success. Parents play an important role in helping their children learn to establish a more robust understanding—one that has more to do with fulfilling their created potential as social beings rather than personal achievements. Thus, some of the practical considerations covered in this chapter include selecting a major, mission trips, service-learning, studies abroad, and vocational discernment.

Chapter Six, "A Time to Cry: Crisis and the College Experience"
Movie: *Higher Learning* (1995)

Crisis events have become all too common in educational institutions, and Christian colleges and universities are not immune. Eating disorders, emotional duress, self-mutilation, and sexual harassment can befall students at colleges and universities regardless of their religious affiliation. Parents need to be aware of the warning signs being demonstrated by their children and their children's friends, and should encourage these young people to be mindful of the warning signs as well. Some of the practical concerns covered in this chapter include campus disaster plans, campus safety or campus police offices, crime statistics, counseling services, disciplinary procedures, and health services.

Chapter Seven, "The Cultivated Vocation: Expectations of Life after Graduation" Movie: *St. Elmo's Fire* (1985)

If the college years are viewed as a time of transition to adulthood, graduation is viewed as a time when a student's understanding of her or himself as an adult solidifies. By viewing Christian college students as more than just people preparing to fulfill necessary functions in society, we see the final year of college as a time when students begin to anticipate the commitments they will be called to fulfill as members of the body of Christ. Thus, some of the practical considerations covered in this chapter include applying to graduate and/or professional schools, applying for jobs, and capstone courses.

A Word of Thanks

We could not have written this book without the support of a number of people. The first two groups we wish to thank include our students, past and present, and their parents. We have learned immeasurably from our relationships with them. We have had the pleasure of meeting parents whom we thought worthy of emulating in our own parenting practices and students whom we felt blessed to have introduced to our own children. While this book draws upon the literature accumulated over years of research, the heart of it is really drawn from the wisdom we gained from these relationships.

We would like to thank several friends who were gracious enough to read drafts of this manuscript: Chris Abrams, Philip Byers, Dave Downey, Polly Graham, Dave Johnstone, Kimberly Thornbury, Susanna Poucher, and Mark Troyer. Philip Byers, Dave Downey, Polly Graham, Sarah Hightower, and Ben Taylor also helped with the research. Elaine Cooper and Sara Ream made some valuable edits that greatly increased the quality of the writing. While the strengths in what you will read are much to their credit, any deficiencies are undoubtedly our own. They were gracious enough to lend their time and wisdom to this project. To them, we are grateful.

Such a project would have proven impossible without the love and support of our church families, Jerome Christian Church and Upland Community Church. In those two contexts, we learned what it means to experience Christian community truly and thus the importance of offering our lives in praise and worship to God and God alone.

Our children, Addison Ream, Ashley Ream, Megan (Herrmann) Kraftson, Matthew Herrmann, Emily Herrmann, Libby Trudeau, Maddy Trudeau, Gabby Trudeau, Kitty Trudeau, and Sam Trudeau, bring a joy in our lives we cannot begin to describe. With all of you, we have learned (despite our fallen nature) the importance of giving glory to God through our efforts as parents. We view each one of you as a special gift God shared with us. We hope more than anything that we have served you well.

Our wives, Sara Ream, Kathy Herrmann, and Jennifer Trudeau, prove to be the partners in our lives for whom we could never have dreamed of asking. You have blessed us, our children, and the countless students whom you welcomed as guests into our homes. We thank you for your love, your support, and your willingness to partner with us in this journey.

This book is dedicated to our parents, Charles and Linda Ream, Bob and Ruthe Herrmann, and Craig and Carole Trudeau. Your willingness to aid in our callings yielded blessings we can never repay except to try to do the same for our own children. From you, we first learned to be parents. As a result, all we can do is say thank you and hope that what follows is a worthy expression of our appreciation.

Greentown, Indiana & Upland, Indiana
First Week in Ordinary Time, 2011

PART I

THE DOMAINS OF COLLEGE LIFE

Where Two or Three Are Gathered

The Centrality of Common Worship

An ivy-draped Princeton University provides an awe-inspiring backdrop to Ron Howard's film, *A Beautiful Mind*. Starring Russell Crow as John Nash, this film bears witness to the firm hand the Cold War placed on the American frame of mind during the 1950s. The film opens with a group of young doctoral students in mathematics sitting through an orientation speech given by the department chair. As the leader of the department, this professor challenges each student to think about what contribution he (the department was all men at that time) will make to the field of mathematics and to the fate of a nation engulfed in this crisis. Mathematicians, he argues, provided many of the technological breakthroughs necessary for the United States and the Allies to emerge victorious from World War II. Now the next generation of mathematicians must take its place against a new enemy, the Soviet Union.

This masterful film goes on to follow the career of John Nash, the man identified by one of his classmates as the "mysterious West Virginia genius." Although brilliant, Nash proves to be socially awkward—once referring to himself as having a chip on both shoulders. Over time, Princeton's hyper-competitive environment accelerates some of the challenges Nash faces. As an outcome of his life-long battle with mental illness, Nash now becomes obsessed with finding his original scholarly idea in his chosen field of mathematics. At one point, Nash breaks down and questions his worth as a whole if he is unable to use his mental gifts at the highest level. Princeton appears to do little to redirect this impression, pitting its students against one another with their cognitive gifts as the weapons.

In the end, Nash discovers his original idea in governing dynamics. His discovery allows him to finish at the top of his class and receive a placement at MIT's Wheeler Laboratories. Nash then goes on to meet his wife, Alicia (played by Jennifer Connolly), who stands by his side through his ongoing challenges with mental illness. The movie closes with Nash winning the Nobel Prize and attributing his success to the love of his wife.

A Beautiful Mind won four Academy Awards and has many inspiring qualities. While critics have noted that the film possesses various historical inconsistencies, my deepest concerns over this film are not so much focused on its treatment of Nash's life but on its portrayal of life at Princeton University. The recurring theme of a singular focus on the mind and on individual competition raises two questions. First, is the college experience (or, in this case, the graduate experience) solely focused on the cultivation of the mind and not a broader set of qualities that define what it means to be human? Second, is the worth of each student measured by his or her individual performance? On many campuses, the answer to both of these questions is yes. However, perhaps the Christian college is different. Perhaps the Christian college says that students are more than just minds. Perhaps the Christian college says that God has called all of us to far more important purposes than just competition with one another.

The Significance of the Christian College

We human beings are, if nothing else, creatures defined by what we desire. Our desires are not simply matters of the mind but also of our body, our emotions, and, most of all, our spirit. The nature of these claims can be found in practically every commercial we see or hear. Producers of products ranging from personal hygiene to home furnishings buy time and share with us their secularized message of salvation tailored to meet our needs (real or perceived). If I just buy this brand of deodorant, I will be able to date a girl who looks like the one in the commercial. If I just buy this living room set, my home will be transformed into the kind of sanctuary where my soul can be restored at the end of a weary day. While neither deodorant nor a living room set can truly provide what their ads promise, the claims they make on our lives confirm that human beings are engaged in a relentless search for what can provide salvation. Material needs are part of the reality in which we live and must never be ignored. But material matters alone cannot provide the kind of peace that even the most well crafted advertisements promise.

Augustine, one of the most well known of the Church Fathers, recognized that human beings are, by their nature, creatures of desire. His *Confessions*, a beautiful work detailing his own Christian conversion, speaks of the restlessness that comes through putting too great a faith in material matters. Augustine recounts the various ways he relied on material things to satisfy his seemingly never-ending desires. Intellectual pursuits, sexual encounters, and cultic religious practices were all exhausted, yet Augustine's desiring nature still haunted him. At the end of this secular pilgrimage, Augustine comes to the point where salvation in Christ and the worship of God alone provide him with peace. Setting the tone for this autobiographical work, Augustine opens by offering that "Our hearts are restless until they rest in Thee, O Lord."[1] In essence, human beings are creatures of desire who only find rest in the worship of their Creator.

The church's central role in the lives of believers is to guide and ground our desires as human beings. New members are initiated into the body of Christ through the act of baptism, our old selves dying in order to be born anew into the Body of Christ. Being born anew does not mean that our desires for material matters disappear entirely. However, being born anew breaks these chains and allows us to begin to have our desires reordered by the power of God's grace. The Apostle Paul writes, "Or don't you know that all of us who were baptized into Christ Jesus were baptized into his death? We were therefore buried with him through baptism into death in order that, just as Christ was raised from the dead through the glory of the Father, we too may live a new life" (Romans 6:3-4). Baptism lays claim on all that defines us—our minds, our bodies, our emotions, and our spirits—in a way that barely makes any distinction between them. In addition, baptism connects our desires and our sense of well-being to the well-being of others. The Apostle Paul again writes, "There is one body and one Spirit—just as you were called to one hope when you were called—one Lord, one faith, one baptism; one God and Father of all, who is over all and through all and in all" (Ephesians 4:4-6). The needs of my neighbor become real and immediate to me if for no other reason than that my neighbor and I are joined as members of the body of Christ.

What we hear in the reading and study of Scripture, we experience by participating in the Lord's Supper. Called by our Lord and Savior to take the bread as his body and the wine as his blood, we are reminded that God's grace and God's grace alone sustains us. Grace does not simply transform our minds, but our bodies, emotions, and spiritual well-being. The Apostle Paul admonishes: "Therefore, I urge you, brothers, in view of God's mercy, to offer your bodies as living sacrifices, holy and pleasing to God—this is your spiritual act of worship. Do not conform any longer to the pattern of this world, but be transformed by the renewing of your mind. Then you will be able to test and approve what God's will is—his good, pleasing and perfect will" (Romans 12:1-2). In addition, grace is not simply a personal gift we can hold in reserve as some kind of commodity. By accepting the sacrifice that made this grace possible, we are called to go forth and share God's grace with others.

As an institution that receives the essence of its identity from the church, the Christian college most readily lives out its mission when it gathers together for common worship. Depending upon the campus, such experiences go by different names and are expressed in different ways. Most campuses will have a common worship experience where all or almost all of the campus gathers together. Some Christian colleges meet twice a week. Others meet three times a week. Some colleges require students to attend a certain number of sessions each semester. Other colleges identify these experiences as optional.

These larger-scale services are then supported by any number of other common worship experiences—for example, morning and evening prayer, Bible studies, and praise and worship times. Regardless of how these experiences are structured, they should be at the center of the Christian college life as reminders that we are called to offer praise and worship to God above all else.

The goal of common worship is for students to learn that, while the cultivation of their minds is important, it cannot be accomplished if the Christian college does not also cultivate a student's body, emotions, and spiritual life. These dimensions of human existence cannot exist apart from one another. For example, a student comes to a Christian college believing she is called to be an artist. When asked why she believes she is called to be an artist, she cannot simply say that a list of pros and cons determined that the best possible option for her was to be an artist. In reality, she not only rationally believes she has been given a certain set of skills, but she recognizes that she has a passion for art. Fulfilling her vocation or calling to serve as an artist becomes something compelling that goes beyond mere rational explanation. The whole of her created identity is geared to serve as an artist. As Parker Palmer, a contemporary writer on education, echoes, "'vocation is something I can't not do, for reasons I'm unable to explain to anyone else and don't fully understand myself but that are nonetheless compelling.'"[2] Common worship confirms that such a calling lays claim on all of who we are, not just a portion.

In addition, common worship is central to the experience of the Christian college because it shows that student a purpose for her artistic calling. She is not simply called to create works of art as a way to prove her supremacy over her fellow artists.

Competition is not the end goal; even so, this young artist is called to perform at as high a level as her created identity will allow. Her reference point for excellence is raised to include the best art she can create given the talents God gave her. She is to create art that reflects her baptism, reflects her participation in the biblical account of creation, fall, and redemption, and reflects her presence at the Lord's Table. She is also called to use her gifts in service to others—to bring beauty into places where there is horror, oppression, and sorrow. While her art may fetch a high price in the auction houses of New York City and London, the price is not why she produces it and not even the ultimate indicator of its true worth. Bringing glory to God by reflecting God and serving others is the reason she produces it, and its worth is measured by God's pleasure.

By placing common worship at the center of the college experience, the Christian college affirms its responsibility to form the identity of students in ways that prepare them to offer their lives in praise and worship of God. As artists and accountants, as physicians and physicists, and as spouses and parents, students should find in their Christian college experience constant reminders of God's calling. Common worship will guide and ground their human desires, cultivating their mental, emotional, and spiritual lives.

What Does the Literature Say?

The second original statute of Harvard University, America's oldest institution of higher learning, declares, "Every one shall consider the main End of his life and studies, to know God and Jesus Christ which is Eternal life."[3] This declaration is consistent with the understandings of virtually all American colleges founded before 1860. Even though modern higher education may no longer be centered on the faith-development of college students and certainly lacks the clearly Christian orientation of Harvard's original charter, it would be a mistake to think that the spirituality of college students is no longer of interest. Alexander Astin, a higher education scholar and the founding director of the Higher Education Research Institute (HERI) at UCLA, addressed the question: "Is Spirituality a Legitimate Concern in Higher Education?" He argues that "even a cursory look at our educational system makes it clear that the relative amount of attention that we devote to the 'exterior' and 'interior' aspects of our lives has gotten way out of balance. Thus, while we are justifiably proud of our 'outer' development in fields such as science, medicine, technology, and commerce, we have increasingly come to neglect our 'inner' development— the sphere of values and beliefs, emotional maturity, spirituality, and self understanding."[4]

Astin is not alone in these convictions. A tremendous resurgence in attention to religion and spirituality in the academy has occurred in recent years. Alan Wolfe, a self-proclaimed "secular academic," believes that "there are at least two reasons to welcome, rather than to ignore, the revival of religion in the academy: Religion can extend the pluralism that liberal values cherish, and it can expand and enrich knowledge."[5] Further evidence of this interest appears in a nationwide study of spirituality conducted by HERI. This project surveyed 112,000 students and 65,000 faculty in an attempt to "document how students change spiritually and religiously during the college years, and to identify the ways in which colleges can contribute to this developmental process."[6]

While interest in spirituality has increased dramatically, we must also recognize that this enhanced attention is not directed toward an orthodox Christian understanding of spirituality. Patrick Love and Donna Talbot, two noted higher education theorists, describe a spirituality that "acknowledge[s] a wide range of belief systems that may or may not incorporate organized religions."[7] Their work, often cited in the literature on college student spirituality, holds that spirituality involves five processes:

- An internal process of seeking personal authenticity, genuineness, and wholeness as an aspect of identity development;
- The process of continually transcending one's current locus of centricity;
- Developing a greater connectedness to self and others through relationships and union with community;
- Deriving meaning, purpose, and direction in one's life; and
- An increasing openness to exploring a relationship with an intangible and pervasive power or essence that exists beyond human existence and rational human knowing.[8]

While this conception of spirituality is not necessarily hostile to Christianity, neither is it congruent with it. The current focus distinguishes between "spirituality" and "religion" with the latter being understood as a formalized expression of a structured belief system.[9] Thus, some scholars suggest that a student may be "spiritual" without being aligned with any formal religious belief system.

Despite the popularity of this view, it is not strongly borne out by the research. In an extensive investigation of first-year students, researchers Alyssa Bryant, Jeung Yun Choi, and Maiko Yasuno found that there was indeed a strong connection between "religiousness and spirituality."[10] In this same study, they found that while students participated less in religious activities during their first year, their desire to incorporate spirituality into their lives increased.

Using this introduction as a backdrop, let's consider the beliefs of America's college students. According to the results of the HERI spirituality survey, eighty percent have an interest in spirituality, seventy-six percent describe themselves as searching for meaning or purpose in life, and sixty-four percent see their spirituality as a source of joy. "Almost eight in ten believe in God, with more than half perceiving God as 'love' or as the 'creator,' and about half experiencing God as a 'protector.'"[11] While these figures show that students have not lost their basic interest in spiritual things, psychology professor Jean Twenge describes the faith that they adhere to, even the faith of evangelical Christians, as "a very personalized form of religion,"[12] one which is highly individualistic and which is very limited in the demands it places on its adherents.

So then, one might reasonably ask, where does the Christian college fit in this picture? Does it make a difference if a student attends a Christian college, and if so, what are the differences? Christian students on Christian college campuses, like their unbelieving counterparts at other types of institutions, enter a critical period of identity development. During these years, students mature in a number of areas that impact their identity. Noted higher education theorists Arthur

Chickering and Linda Reisser recognize the development of competence, emotional management, the establishment of independence and the move toward interdependence, growth in the capacity to engage in mature relationships, the development of a sense of purpose, and the growth of integrity as the crucial elements of identity development in college students.[13] Not only is each one of these areas critical for the cultivation of maturity, each one is impacted by the college experience. The college years are also a period during which religious identity evolves as students reassess and either reject, alter, or embrace the beliefs with which they were raised.

According to developmental psychologist James Marcia, students may deal with challenges to their beliefs in several ways during this period. Those students who simply adopt the beliefs of their parents because that is what they were raised with are referred to as being "foreclosed." These individuals may know exactly what they believe but would be hard pressed to defend their beliefs or explain why they hold them. As parents, we may initially be comforted that our children believe what we do. If they have arrived at this point without critical examination, however, without testing, and without seriously evaluating alternatives, they are prone to develop a brittle faith which is unlikely to hold up to the difficult challenges that life and, perhaps, even college will throw at them.

In contrast, some young people not only have not critically evaluated what they believe but have not even seriously considered those beliefs. They live according to their whims and whatever serves their perceived interests at any given moment. These students, termed "diffused" by Marcia, are not really even making a serious attempt to solidify their beliefs and do not have an identity foundation to guide their values, beliefs, or decisions. These students are likely to be swayed easily or disengaged from any serious pursuit of the important things in life.

Many students are seriously pursuing truth and evaluating what they believe but have not yet committed themselves to acting on a particular set of beliefs. These students, in a state of identity "moratorium," may be characterized by the U2 lyric: "I still haven't found what I'm looking for." They sincerely desire truth and are honestly searching but have not yet gathered enough "evidence" to allow themselves to make a firm decision and commitment.

Marcia's final category is identity "achievement," and it refers to young people who have seriously evaluated and tested what they believe and have committed to a course of action that reflects those beliefs. This category is consistent with Chickering and Reisser's idea of integrity. Although we may think of integrity as simply telling the truth, this idea goes far beyond the nature of our words. It implies that one's words as well as one's lifestyle, choices, and values are consistent with one's stated beliefs, and it is related to the biblical concept of faithfulness. While, of course, no person's life reflects perfect integrity or congruence, the individual whose identity is "achieved" will show a general consistency in all areas of her or his life.[14]

These basic developmental issues raise an important question. If these challenges are occurring in the lives of students, what is the college's role in nurturing optimal development? The answer to this question is complex and strongly related to the way an institution views its students. Institutions that see their students as unique creations with an ultimate sense of purpose as well as the potential to serve others and further God's kingdom will approach education differently than institutions that see students as the sum of their biological parts or simply the highest form of animal life. Because of this commitment, Christian colleges are uniquely positioned to help students confront these challenges. It would not be fair or wise to expect public institutions to support a student's Christian faith development. While many Christians thrive in their faith at secular or non-orthodox faith-based institutions, clearly some falter, especially those students whose faith is immature or otherwise not well founded.

Consider the possible ramifications of a Christian college education for identity development. Under ideal circumstances, *foreclosed* students are challenged to consider why they believe what they do and why they have rejected certain beliefs and values. *Diffused* students are challenged by the community, curriculum, and co-curriculum to examine their lives and beliefs in order to begin moving toward a commitment to beliefs and actions that will result in a life well-lived, a life that matters. Students in *moratorium* are challenged by ideas and experiences as well as the lives of staff and fellow students to move toward a commitment to a belief system and an accompanying way of life. And, finally, students whose identity has been *achieved* are challenged to follow through on commitments, to strive for greater clarity of beliefs, and to live out their faith more fully.

While no serious practitioner would characterize the Christian college as an idyllic place where every student is optimally nurtured toward growth and a solid faith, the environment clearly has tremendous potential to help students grow toward maturity and toward stronger faith. Steve Beers,

Vice President for Student Life at John Brown University, outlines the primary faith dimensions that should be addressed in Christian higher education. Furthermore, he advocates that the following items are particularly well suited to be addressed through common worship. According to Beers, the Christian college ultimately wants each student to:

- Trust in God's saving grace and believe firmly in the humanity and divinity of Jesus;
- Experience a sense of personal well-being, security, and peace;
- Integrate faith and life, seeing work, family, social relationships, and political choices as part of one's Christian life;
- Seek spiritual growth through study, reflection, prayer, and discussion with others;
- Seek to be part of a community of believers in which people give witness to their faith and support and nourish one another;
- Hold life-affirming values including commitment to racial and gender equality, affirmation of cultural and religious diversity, and a personal sense of responsibility for the welfare of others;
- Advocate social and global change to bring about greater social justice; and
- Serve humanity, consistently and passionately, through acts of love and justice.[15]

Although accomplishing these tasks is no small feat, the commitment to pursuing them is a critical element of Christian higher education. While Christian colleges do not have a corner on the faith development of young people, one cannot take Christian higher education seriously without giving concerted attention to the pursuit of these goals.

What Can Parents Do?

What role should parents play in supporting spiritual formation of their daughter or son at a Christian college? A starting point is realizing just how integral common worship is to the overall college experience. One of the hallmarks of Christian higher education is integrating biblical truth into the curriculum and co-curriculum. Chapel as the means for common worship, gathering, and faith development is a critical component. This is historically true of Christian colleges where chapel services have always been a part of the program and have been viewed as a litmus test for a school's spiritual vitality.[16] It is also true for the contemporary Christian college, as chapel services unite the campus culture around current religious issues as well as provide meaningful times of worship and the embrace of a shared Christian identity. These experiences are vitally important to the biblical pursuit found in the book of Romans, which calls its readers not to "conform any longer to the pattern of this world, but be transformed by the renewing of your mind. Then you will be able to test and approve what God's will is— his good, pleasing and perfect will" (Romans 12:2).

In fact, corporate worship and gathering may be more critical for this current generation of students than for previous ones. Students today have been given several labels including Millenials,[17] Generation Q,[18] and the Organizational Kid.[19] All of these labels attempt to capture the essence of this current generation, and all do to some degree. However, Scott Seider

and Howard Gardner have given a new label to this generation, one that has particular importance to our discussion. They
have labeled the current group of students the "Fragmented
Generation."[20] They describe the current generation as having
"grown up in a fragmented America" and assert that "their
identities are more fragmented than those of any previous
group in American history."[21] Some attributes that they ascribe
to this fragmented generation include a reliance on Wikipedia
and other online sources as significant and ultimate sources
of truth, an inability to identify significant heroes or mentors
in their lives, and a tendency to exist in multiple worlds and
identities via online services such as Facebook, MySpace, and
Second Life.[22]

This is a somewhat unsettling description when coupled
with the findings outlined by David Kinnamon and Gabe
Lyons of the Barna Group in their book *unChristian*. Their
research points to the growing disillusionment of sixteen- to
twenty-five-year-olds with traditional religious institutions
and authority.[23] This information should provide, at the very
least, a wakeup call to parents concerned with the spiritual
development and education of their children in this age group
as well as to those of us involved in Christ-centered higher
education. Although their book focuses primarily on nonbe-
lievers, there is a growing sense that their descriptions also
apply to members of the Fragmented Generation who align
themselves with Christianity. Consider Kinnamon and Lyons'
depiction of this generation:

> Spirituality is important to young adults, but many
> consider it just one element of a successful, eclectic

life. Fewer than one out of ten young adults mention faith as their top priority, despite the fact that the vast majority of Busters and Mosaics attended a Christian church during their high school years. Most young people who were involved in church as a teenager disengage from church life and often from Christianity at some point during early adulthood creating a deficit of young talent, energy, and leadership in many congregations.[24]

What can we take from these gloomy descriptions of today's college students? The bad news is that they are disillusioned with traditional church activities and are not as likely to engage as readily as previous generations. The good news is that they are also very interested in spirituality and are seeking means to establish their religious identities. The key seems to be finding appropriate avenues where foundational Christianity is presented in a manner that embraces and honors the historical Jesus of the Bible while remaining vibrant and relevant to this generation. Chapel or corporate worship is not the only method of helping a fragmented and disillusioned generation find identity within a biblical educational context, but it should be seen as one very important element.

Corporate worship plays a critical role in helping this generation find unity, purpose, and identity within the body of Christ. It is one of the primary goals of Christian higher education, and knowing this can enable parents to assist in their child's transition to college. Common worship or chapel is as important an element as academic programs, campus location, and tuition costs when considering Christian colleges.

Since many Christian liberal arts colleges offer similar core programs, comparing chapel programs may provide a unique perspective on the differences between schools. The following section provides some practical advice on how to support your children in this process.

I am a strong proponent of making campus visits during the process of choosing a college. Try to visit on a day when chapel is held so you can experience it first-hand. Observe how engaged students are with the program. Look around you; are students actively listening and participating in corporate worship, or are they distracted and doing other things like sleeping, talking, or reviewing notes for their next class? Take note of whether students are involved in the program itself, whether in the music, leading the service, or speaking. In my experience, the more students are involved in chapel services, the more active and engaged other students will be. You will be surprised by what you can glean from these simple observations.

In addition to attending chapel, ask about the program. Talk to students and college personnel and have them describe how they experience chapel. Chapel is an experience shared by almost everyone on a Christian college campus, so you should be able to get several perspectives. Review a complete schedule of speakers and special programs to get an idea of the breadth and depth of the program. Some schools now make their chapel programs available online or have an archive of past chapels so you can gain a broader perspective.

Once you have experienced chapel and asked for a variety of perspectives, make sure you discuss it with your daughter or son, preferably as soon as you can so the images and thoughts will be fresh. The car ride home would be the ideal time. Ask how your child experienced the program and what current students told her or him about how they experience chapel. Share your perceptions and what you heard others say. This kind of discussion will allow you to add chapel considerations to the overall decision-making process. Again, chapel will not necessarily make or break the Christian college experience but it is central to the experience and is therefore worthy of significant attention in the decision-making process.

There are several aspects of chapel to include in your discussions. Two important ones are the relationship of chapel to regular church attendance and involvement, and the style of worship in chapel and the topics presented. These two topics are important in helping students develop a healthy spiritual life while at college as well as preparing them to understand the differences between a college chapel and their home church.

Regular attendance in chapel, although important to a student's spiritual life and education, is not a substitute for finding a church home. At every Christian college with which I am familiar, there are a variety of local churches and many opportunities for students to get involved. In many instances, these churches actively seek to attract college students to their services. Often they provide transportation to and from campus or compile a network of other students and members who can provide rides. In addition, many of these churches have specific programs for college students and provide opportunities for ministry in the local community. Getting involved in a local church is imperative, and chapel, though spiritually beneficial, does not replace the need for a church home while at college.

Two of the most frequent reasons I hear from students who don't go to chapel are "I don't like the style of worship" and "Chapel services are so different from my home church and I just can't get into them." Even when attending a college affiliated with their own denomination, students should expect chapel services to be different from what they are used to at home. Good chapel programs seek to represent the broader context of evangelicalism as opposed to a more narrow denominational approach. On any Christian college campus, there will be a wide variety of church traditions represented in the student body, and chapel services will at times be unlike what your children are used to and may require them to step out of their comfort zone. Exposing students to a variety of worship styles is an important educational experience, helping them gain broader insights into their own faith and the body of Christ. Chapel is an ideal time for multiple cultural perspectives to be presented in a respectful, integrated environment. This type of diversity can broaden a student's faith perspective while at the same time helping to strengthen personal convictions.

Parental support for chapel should continue after your child has enrolled. Ask occasionally how chapel services are going, who spoke, how the worship was, and whether your child is attending. Parents can often download recordings of chapel services from the college's Web site. These conversations will allow her another opportunity to reflect on what she has experienced and to cultivate an understanding of how those learning experiences relate to her faith. These discussions can also provide valuable insights into how well your child's overall experience is going.

If students are engaged with the chapel program, they are more likely to be engaged with other aspects of Christian college life. Help your daughter or son realize that chapel is good spiritually, educationally, and socially. Common worship helps students weave their academic work with their belief system, and shows them how intellectual studies can ultimately be glorifying to God.

Conclusion

Unfortunately, John Nash and the Princeton he attended are probably not alone in the conviction that the college experience is only about the cultivation of the mind. While the cultivation of the mind is certainly central to the Christian college experience, it must be understood in the context of its place in the cultivation of the heart and soul. As a result, the experience of common worship becomes central to the formative influence offered by a Christian education, creating an integrated understanding of what it means to be part of human society and of the body of Christ.

PENCILS DOWN, TIME'S UP

The Nature of the Classroom

Like *A Beautiful Mind*, *Mona Lisa Smile* is set in the mid 1950s. Instead of an all-male Princeton, *Mona Lisa Smile* is set at equally majestic, Wellesley College. An institution dedicated to the education of women, Wellesley's spires and ivy-draped halls rival any other campus in the country, and its level of academic rigor is second to none. While this film is set during the Cold War, the students at Wellesley—unlike those in *A Beautiful Mind*—are not committed to using their gifts and talents to subdue the threat of global Communism. Rather, they are preparing to assume their places as the spouses of those leading that charge. The students at Wellesley were believed to be the brightest group of young women to be found anywhere, but they were there to learn their roles as housewives and servants to their husbands.

The tension between Wellesley's identity as a finishing school and its identity as a college offers the backdrop for what would unfold during the 1953-1954 academic year. A young art historian, Katherine Watson (played by Julia Roberts), comes to Wellesley that year and forms a unique relationship with members of the senior class. As a first-year faculty member from

California, Watson quickly realizes that her students know the material but cannot process it or appreciate its significance. On the first day of class, Watson runs out of material because her students had already read and committed to memory the content of both the primary and secondary readings for the course. On the second day of class, Watson comes prepared, not with more material, but with a battery of questions requiring the students to assess the content they had mastered. When faced with questions without prescribed answers, the students appeared perplexed, almost unable to respond.

One of the turning points in the film comes when Watson takes her class to a warehouse (apparently in Boston) where a Jackson Pollack painting is being uncrated. Watson stands before the painting, almost entranced, and strives to appreciate its unique qualities. Repelled by the painting's modern sensibilities, several of the students begin to make jokes. Watson quickly rebukes them, arguing that while they are not required to like the painting, they are required to consider it. They are required to stand before it, take in all it has to offer, and then offer some assessment of its value as a work of art. Learning from their teacher, the students then stand before the painting, becoming entranced as well, seeking to grasp what this painting has to offer. Appreciation for art thus becomes more than simply learning to whom to attribute a particular painting and its date of completion. It becomes something requiring that the full identity of these young women (their moral identity, their physical identity, and arguably even their spiritual identity) be utilized in that process.

Although the film is to be applauded for its argument that learning at the college level demands more than simply the cognitive mastery of facts, it fails to understand why this type of learning is so important when one is pursuing an overarching goal. In an editorial in the year-end issue of the student newspaper, one student admiringly writes that Watson had taught her and her peers to "Seek truth beyond tradition, beyond definition, beyond image." Her tribute to her teacher is inspiring, but misses the point that the search for truth is not something that takes place in a vacuum. Rather, the search for truth is guided by a certain goal or aspiration—what Neil Postman has called "the end of education."[1]

The Significance of the Classroom

Mona Lisa Smile was right to challenge the view that a college education was only about an intellectual mastery over a certain set of facts. However, the film fails to appreciate the full significance of the context in which a college education takes place. I am referring to the classroom as that context here, but it could also include the library, the laboratory, the studio, the field station, or even the residence hall (as I will argue in chapter three)—anywhere active learning takes place. For the Christian college, our identity as Christians sets the goal for the efforts that take place in these contexts. Writing a paper, practicing the piano, or conducting a chemistry experiment— all of these efforts are various ways students learn to offer praise and worship to God.

Too often, we applaud students merely for exhibiting curiosity in academic settings. The rationale driving a film like *Mona Lisa Smile* is that a college education is best undertaken in contexts where students understand the relative nature of truth and are free to follow their curiosity wherever it may lead. The downfall of this way of thinking is that learning remains directionless and thus dependent upon the will and the worldview of the individual student. The contexts in which active learning takes place at a Christian college are designed to deepen the appreciation of students for how they can offer praise and worship of God. God is glorified by a well-crafted poem. God is glorified by an appreciation for the chemical intricacies of the created order. God is glorified by a well-played piano sonata. God is glorified by the recognition that God, not the student, is the one who made such efforts possible. The student is simply learning to become a steward of those gifts.

If the classroom, the laboratory, the library, the recital hall, the studio, and even the residence hall are contexts in which active learning takes place, then the various academic disciplines provide the means for that learning. Literature, philosophy, music, and economics are means by which students learn to appreciate God's world. It is one thing to listen to or read a well-written poem; it is another to learn the discipline it takes to write the poem. Because offering praise and worship of God makes demands on the whole person, active learning experiences should do the same. For example, chemistry should not be reduced simply to learning various chemical exchanges. Rather, it should also provoke the awe and wonder of a student learning to appreciate some of the very foundations of the created order. It should encourage the student to consider the moral implications of caring for this world. It should make the student realize that he or she is not simply a passive observer but an active participant in this order.

Well-designed course requirements at a Christian college are set to order students' desires in this very direction. Most often, the foundation of this course design is referred to as general education or the core curriculum. Some students ask why they are forced to take courses they believe do not directly relate to their major or anticipated career. The answer is that these courses are required because they provide a foundation for seeing the world in richer, fuller ways.

General education or core curriculum courses come mostly from what are called the liberal arts. The term "liberal" does not refer to current political and social views, but to the qualities these courses are believed to produce. In the case of the Christian college, these qualities include a growing ability to appreciate the fullness of God's creation. For example, a student majoring in economics may not understand why he is required to take two literature courses. However, the study of literature introduces him to the reality that we all live within certain stories or traditions. How we view the world, and what we believe to be true and untrue, are formed by these stories. Literature teaches us not only to understand our own stories and those of others, but also how these stories support and/or contradict God's great story of creation, fall, and redemption. Courses in foreign languages, history, mathematics, philosophy, theology—courses which often make up general education requirements—are designed to produce similar effects.

In addition to core courses required of all students, almost all colleges allow students to select a major as well as several elective courses. For many students, selecting a major can prove daunting, almost comparable to getting married: "If I major in nursing, I must then be a nurse for the rest of my life. If so, how do I know for sure I am ready to make such a commitment?" In reality, the selection of a major is hardly ever a lifelong commitment. The present state of the American workplace suggests that students will need to be prepared to enter several different careers over the course of their lifetimes. In addition, more and more students each year are finding that graduate work is necessary to secure the types of jobs they desire. Often, this coursework is not in an area directly related to their undergraduate major. As a result, the best way to select a major is to simply consider what course of study will best exercise one's gifts and created talents so that one can give glory to God.

If the classroom is the context and the disciplines are the means to pursuing that calling, what role do professors play? Too often (as was critiqued in *Mona Lisa Smile*), professors are perceived to be experts in a given field who dispense irrefutable facts. One common label for such a professor is the "sage on the stage." Certainly, professors should be active scholars and experts in their fields. But professors with even a modest amount of humility will readily admit that their knowledge is far from complete. They know that learning is a never-ending process of appreciating the created order. As a result, professors are called to serve your daughters and sons as mentors—not just introducing them to a field of study but also serving as role models and guides on a common journey. Learning is a constant process of vision and revision, of striving to appreciate something in its full detail only to realize that some important elements have slipped through our grasp. As in the movie *Mona Lisa Smile*, professors, by their very example, must challenge students to consider every aspect of the world around them. But at a Christian college, professors are called to do more—to serve as role models and guides in a common area of study that can, in the end, deepen a student's ability to praise and worship God.

If providing expert information is only one part of a professor's role, what then are the others? One is to invite students to participate in practices that eventually form good academic habits. A foundation for practically all disciplines is reading. The professor has the responsibility of requiring a volume of reading that may be a little beyond the student's current ability and written at a depth beyond which they are accustomed. The goal is not to overwhelm students, but to challenge them, to cultivate habits that represent a higher level of self-discipline than they currently have. Students may view such professors as burdensome or too demanding. In reality, as long as the professor is a willing role model, working alongside students, this expectation is grounded in the hope of nurturing students' potential. When selecting courses and professors, too many students choose paths of least resistance. In the end, these students sell themselves short as their academic habits remained unchallenged and never expand. An "A" earned with minimal effort helps a student less in the long run than a "B" or even a "C" that was harder to achieve. Seeing all of life's challenges as opportunities to offer praise and worship to God will only happen when students learn to embrace those challenges in the first place.

Before I move on to discuss the impact of the classroom on students, perhaps I should offer a few remarks about academic freedom. As portrayed in the movie *Mona Lisa Smile*, too often learning is perceived to best take place in environments free of any larger purpose. While academic freedom is imperative to the success of the Christian college, that term needs clarification. If anything, professors at the Christian college are freer than their counterparts at state universities or private, non-sectarian universities. The source of this freedom comes by virtue of the fact that they are free to pursue a common goal. Although they share in this common purpose, their chosen means, by virtue of the diversity of disciplines they represent, are different.

As participants in the created order, faculty members at the Christian college may very well pursue and even introduce their students to topics that might be controversial or offensive. The reason is not simply to appreciate these topics but to learn to critique and perhaps even redeem them. Engaging material some people find controversial or offensive simply because one can is never a responsible expression of one's calling as a scholar. Many times, students never learn to distinguish between material that is potentially controversial and offensive but possesses serious merit and comparable material that has no redeeming qualities. Professors at the Christian college are called not only to know the difference, but to introduce their students to that material which merits consideration.

Human sexuality is a clear example of a potentially controversial subject for faculty members at a Christian college. When practiced within the context of the marital covenant, it is a beautiful gift of God. However, perhaps no element of God's created order has been impacted by the fall more than sexuality. Conversations from a uniquely Christian perspective are desperately needed in order to redeem what was originally created for good. If professors in courses such as theology, psychology, and biology shy away from such conversations because they might prove controversial, students will inevitably turn to other sources of authority. The critical question, then, is not whether to engage this topic but how and with what purpose in mind.

For the Christian college, the goal of forming within students the desire to offer praise and worship to God is preeminent. Classrooms provide the context for these formative experiences. The academic disciplines provide the means. Finally, professors serve as worthy yet imperfect guides who have been down this path and know that there is more to explore. In this process of never-ending exploration, they invite their students, your sons and daughters, to find their place in God's story of creation, fall, and redemption.

What Does the Literature Say?

Just as the parents of the students in *Mona Lisa Smile* sought the benefits of Wellesley as a finishing school, it is easy for believing parents mistakenly to see Christian colleges as the spiritual equivalent. While we certainly want our daughters and sons to have their faith internalized and strengthened, the educational process that leads to the development of solid, resilient belief may not be as straightforward as we might wish. Viewing the ideal classroom as simply a place where an expert professor pours information into willing, novice students is overly simplistic. Teaching does include the imparting of knowledge, but knowledge that is not processed, prodded, personalized, and applied is retained only briefly and generally has limited usefulness.

As we saw in chapter one, psychologist James Marcia offers an explanation of identity development that may be helpful as we consider the impact of the classroom experience. He asserts that healthy identity is developed and solidified as people deal with crisis and commitment. By "crisis," he is not referring so much to life-altering trauma as he is to meaningful, critical evaluation of what we hold to be true. He argues that until we have conducted a critical evaluation of our convictions and tested them in our experience, we cannot meaningfully commit to a particular belief system. As noted earlier, those who do commit before this evaluation takes place are characterized as "foreclosed." Foreclosure implies the adoption or inheritance of one's beliefs from others. While such beliefs may be very orthodox, the impact of these beliefs on the one holding them is likely to be much more limited than beliefs that are critically examined and tested by doubt. Additionally, when these beliefs are challenged by life's troubles or unsympathetic critics, these students may then lack the strength needed to persist.

The college classroom offers many opportunities for students to test and to think objectively about their convictions in a manner that helps them develop an effective blending of belief and behavior. When considering improvements in principled moral reasoning, evidence suggests that students at colleges with a liberal arts curriculum, one which exposes them to different points of view, ideas, and worldviews, make the greatest gains. In contrast, students at colleges where pre-college beliefs are uncritically reinforced showed the smallest gains in principled moral reasoning.[2] In fact, being forced to examine and integrate one's beliefs seems to have a significant impact on the ability to apply those beliefs to help solve moral dilemmas.

The practice of objectively considering one's beliefs carries implications far beyond the spiritual realm. While the purpose of a literature, history, or biology course is not specifically moral or identity development, the process of learning requires a student to critically examine information in order to comprehend it and put it to use. Of course, at Christian colleges, there is a significant amount of content in many academic fields that relates directly to personal beliefs and biblical content. Perhaps more importantly, the foundation of Christian education and inquiry is that "all truth is God's truth."[3] Knowing this, it is critical that we do not lose sight of the fact that all knowledge and all learning has theological significance and should be examined critically.

Thoughts of the college classroom may conjure up many memories—some good, some bad. Perhaps you hold images that include visions of a favorite teacher whose stirring lectures stimulated heart and mind, who challenged you to think beyond your own limited perspectives and experiences, and who made you want to work harder and do more. These visions may involve a professor whose caring concern for students gave them the confidence they needed to take risks and embrace the challenges of their college experience. For some, images of the college classroom include frustrating experiences in which underprepared, disinterested, perhaps even arrogant, faculty members droned on incessantly with little apparent concern for the well-being or learning of their students.

Which of these pictures represents the ideal? Of course it is the one in which students are nurtured and stretched and thus equipped to fulfill their callings and to address the needs of the world. In this ideal picture, hearts are changed in a manner that compels students to be their best so that they are best equipped to serve. C. S. Lewis advises us in *The Abolition of Man* that "the task of the modern educator is not to cut down jungles but to irrigate deserts." This metaphor provides an excellent guide for both teachers and students.

One of the exercises I ask my students to engage in is to describe the best teacher they have had. This teacher can come from any realm—from kindergarten to college, from home to Sunday school to the workplace. In almost all cases, the common threads of greatness include clarity and focus, motivation, meaningful content, relevance, and a deep concern for students. While this list does not include every element required for a successful classroom experience, these components are clearly among the keys required to promote active, enthusiastic learning.

Let's consider basic classroom goals. If you examine the general education objectives of almost any college or university in the country, you will find that they seek to promote critical thinking, competent verbal and written communication, civic-mindedness, and lifelong learning. A recent higher education report added "complex problem solving, respect for people different from oneself, principled ethical behavior . . . and teamwork" to this list.[4] These educational aspirations have been found to be a very effective framework for general coursework. Students do report that their strongest learning gains occur in the following areas: their major field; general knowledge; ability to think critically; interpersonal skills; analytical and problem-solving skills; job-related skills; and leadership abilities.[5]

In recent years, there has been a great deal of interest in the classroom practices that most effectively promote student learning. Institutions spend much time trying to find an approach that will promote these educational aspirations and help students grow in areas that may be unique to particular institutions and disciplines. The most important principle and the one most foundational to all learning is actually a concept that is surprisingly, even humorously, simple. This principle is called by several different names but is most commonly labeled "involvement" or "engagement." It says that students learn best about the things to which they give their greatest energy and attention.[6] Thus, the potential benefits of any classroom activity can be measured by simply considering how well it causes students to engage the course material. While choosing these activities may seem out of your child's control, in fact, students have a great deal of control over what takes place in their classroom.

A number of researchers have tried to find just what it is that promotes classroom learning. Several have agreed that in order to be effective, the teacher must: create appropriate levels of challenge; foster a supportive environment in which students can question and explore what they are learning; actively involve students in the learning process; acknowledge a variety of learning styles; expect a lot from students; communicate clear goals and objectives; provide timely feedback on coursework; and, finally, assess the accomplishment of course objectives.[7]

In a very funny sketch, comedian Father Guido Sarducci presents "The Five Minute University."[8] His university is very attractive because the degree only takes five minutes to obtain, costs just $20, and boasts learning results that rival conventional institutions. He spends five minutes explaining his college and covering what he believes the average college graduate remembers five years after graduation. For instance, in the foreign language course students are taught "¿Cómo está usted?" along with the appropriate response, "Muy bien." He argues convincingly that this is all that is needed because five years after graduation "that's really about all you are really going to remember anyway."

Now, while we may laugh at the absurdity of his overstatement, actually his claim is not too far from what the research shows us. According to most of the research, lecturing—still the most common instructional approach among college professors—generally results in very modest recall. Studies typically indicate that only between twenty and fifty percent of lecture material is retained and the higher figure is reached only rarely and very shortly after the lecture is delivered. The farther a student gets from the actual presentation, the less is retained.[9] Clearly, these results do not seem to indicate a value worth the tremendous financial and time output required by a college education. So then, if the most important impact of the classroom experience is not the simple transmission and retention of information, we might rightfully ask, "What is?"

In response, we must be careful not to "throw out the baby with the bath water." While gains in the acquisition of specific information may be relatively modest, they are hardly inconsequential. Students do acquire a considerable amount of information or "subject matter knowledge" during college. "Students not only make significant gains in subject matter knowledge during the undergraduate years but also become more critical, reflective, and sophisticated thinkers."[10] According to a comprehensive review of the research literature, college students make the greatest gains in their ability to analyze, evaluate, and manipulate information ("epistemological sophistication or maturity"), thinking reflectively, and in "liberal arts competencies (for example, using science, using art, solving problems)."[11]

Ultimately, these higher-order thinking skills yield the greatest benefits because they are the tools that assist students in their development of cognitive abilities. These abilities in turn form the foundation for students' future learning endeavors. In other words, these are the skills that allow students to learn how to learn and prepare them to achieve one of the key objectives of a liberal arts experience, namely to become lifelong learners.

Let's look at just one of these, "epistemological sophistication," and think about how it might be beneficial. This impressive sounding phrase can be pretty simply defined as the ability to judge truth claims, evaluate conflicting worldviews, and apply information appropriately. We want our children to possess these skills as young adults, but they do not come from being spoon-fed facts and truths. The simple imparting of information will not achieve the hopes and dreams that we have for our students to be intellectually independent. For this to happen, they must be guided through the evaluation of a wide array of ideas, opinions, and facts. One of the best opportunities for accomplishing this comes through engagement with the rich, complex, and varied content associated with the liberal arts.

Earlier in this chapter I argued that the rationale driving the film *Mona Lisa Smile* is that a college education should allow students to follow their curiosity wherever it may lead. The problem with this view is that learning remains directionless and dependent upon the will of the individual student. We want to guard against this danger. But we also believe that "all truth is God's truth." So when our students exhibit the studiousness to follow where God may lead and when they marvel at the great truths and mystery of the created order, we rejoice.

Christian higher education can guard against the dangers of an unfettered or unfocused curiosity driven by distrust and skepticism by teaching students to accept that an ultimate, knowable reality exists. While we understand that in this life we must strain because we only see "through a glass darkly," we do so with the confidence of the psalmist who proclaims: "The earth is the Lord's, and everything in it, the world, and all who live in it; for he founded it upon the seas and established it upon the waters" (Psalm 24:1-2). Ultimately, the goal is that our students—your daughters and sons—might search for truth in a way that leads them to desire and discover in ways consistent with the Christian narrative of creation, fall, and redemption.

What Can Parents Do?

The fundamental tension found in *Mona Lisa Smile* has been played out in various forms throughout the history of American higher education. In the movie, the tension is whether Wellesley College should prepare these women for a single, predetermined societal role or expose them to an array of intellectual pursuits and thus prepare them for a variety of societal roles. If only it were as easy as Hollywood presents it. How do you as parents help your daughters and sons navigate this tension, support them through the process of choosing a college, and guide them during their college years?

In real life, the contemporary higher education version of this tension is found between those who advocate specific vocational training versus those who support the broad exposure to the world of ideas as preparation for entering society. Is the purpose of a college degree to prepare students for specific jobs or is it to prepare them to face changing societal and vocational demands? The basic question here is "What is the role of liberal arts, specifically, Christian liberal arts?" Unlike the movie, the real life choice is not as clear cut. Students graduating from liberal arts programs need to be vocationally equipped to enter the workforce and intellectually equipped to flourish in a society that requires people who can adapt to rapid changes and solve complex problems.

We have already established that a main goal of higher education is to help students become comfortable in the world of ideas and to equip them to engage the pressing societal issues of the day. I would now like to focus on two fundamental questions the Christian college-bound students and their families need to address. The first is whether a traditional liberal arts education is a viable option, and the second is whether this is the right setting for your child to pursue his or her education. We will explore these two questions and then discuss how you can support your child as she or he participates in all that the classroom has to offer.

Given the nature of this book and my inherent bias, my answer to the first question is simply, "Yes, a liberal arts education is a viable option." This question is a variation of one of the major themes from *Mona Lisa Smile*: whether the female students in the movie should actively engage in learning as inspired by their faculty or meekly prepare to assume the societal roles dictated to them. In other words, the real question was, "What was the purpose of their education?" Here, our question addresses Christian higher education and liberal arts curriculums. Does the pursuit of a liberal arts degree at a Christian college make sense in terms of current educational practices and options and in the context of today's economic crisis?

Possibly the biggest issue in all of higher education today is the consumer-driven demand for increased accountability. Many people feel that for too long, institutions of higher learning have been left to operate unchecked, resulting in ineffective curricula and institutions that are out of touch with the needs of both students and society. The authors of the 2005 report entitled *Accountability for Better Results: A National Imperative for Higher Education* provide the following summary of these accountability questions: "Public interest in accountability is rooted in the growing importance of higher education and uncertainty concerning its adequacy and affordability. We need better results from higher education, and better approaches for accountability are essential."[12]

Specifically regarding the liberal arts, concerns have been raised as to whether graduates are gaining the requisite knowledge and skills demanded by the workplace. Are students really learning during their time on campus or has this become a four-year (or more) gap experience before they enter into more productive roles in society? These concerns are coupled with growing angst over the escalating cost of tuition, causing many families to question their return on investment. They want the college of their choice to make both educational and vocational sense to insure their son's and daughters' future success.

So why do I answer the viability question with an unequivocal yes? Because, even in a strained economy and despite concerns surrounding educational quality, a college degree still results in a greater earning potential. But even more importantly, as noted earlier, students improve in an array of other areas including intellectual skills, psychosocial and moral development, attitudes and values, and in general enjoy a higher quality of life.[13] Sandy Baum and Kathleen Payea, in *The Benefits of Higher Education for Individuals and Society*, report similar benefits for college degree recipients: lower unemployment rates and poverty, fewer health-related issues such as smoking, and higher levels of civic engagement such as voting and volunteerism.[14] In economic terms alone, college graduates are estimated to earn from $800,000[15] to more than $1 million[16] dollars more than non-college graduates over their career life and unemployment rates are much lower for college grads (6.1%) than for those with high school diplomas (19.6%).[17]

The next question is whether the Christian college is the right setting for your daughter or son—and, if the answer is yes, how you decide which one is the right one. Again, my answer to this question is a strong yes. Many Christian colleges provide the benefits of a liberal arts college but have the added dimension of providing these within the context of a nurturing Christian environment where faith can be integrated into the learning process. The inextricable relationship shared by faith and learning[18] has long been the mantra of the Christian college and it is what distinguishes it from other colleges and universities. What better environment to equip students to address the challenges of our times than one that not only allows them to use their faith as a lens to focus and filter their education but facilitates this as a necessary ingredient in this process?

Conclusion

Consider a modern version of the scenario presented in *Mona Lisa Smile*. Your daughter is enrolled in a course with a professor who is presenting new and challenging material that is, in your daughter's description, "way out there" and completely outside "our family's way of thinking." "Professor X is asking me to think and respond in ways that I am not comfortable with and I am not sure if this college was the right choice for me." The way you respond to this as a parent can be critical to your daughter's education. Should you actively listen and encourage your daughter to be open to new ideas? Should you advise your daughter to have a clarifying conversation with the professor to express her concerns? Or should you react immediately, contact the school, and demand attention be given to the heresy being taught by this professor? Obviously, I think you should avoid the latter approach. Instead, take the opportunity to help your daughter reflect appropriately on what she is experiencing. Be careful not to rush to provide answers, but first listen patiently and provide insight when it is appropriate. Finding the balance between supporting her through difficult issues and encouraging her to engage in new experiences and ways of thinking will not be the easiest thing to do, but it is critically important as you continue to nurture your child in college. This is particularly true in the Christian college world where exposure to new ideas is part of cultivating a student's aspiration and ability to live out the ideals of the Christian narrative.

Not All Fun and Games

College beyond the Classroom

Far from the somber and hallowed landscapes of Princeton University and Wellesley College, the fictitious Faber College provides the backdrop to perhaps the most well known college film of all time, *Animal House* (filmed at the University of Oregon). The film opens in the early 1960s as two first-year students make their way through the host of rush parties being offered by the fraternities. These two young men, who would later receive the pledge names of Flounder and Pinto, first make a failed attempt at impressing the members of what is perceived to be the best fraternity on campus. As one member escorts them around the room, they quickly learn that this fraternity is home to the captains of various sports teams, officials in student government, and the editor of the school newspaper. Instead of introducing the two young men to some of these campus leaders, their host eventually leads them to what is known as the "dink room"—a holding cell for young men deemed undesirable.

Frustrated with their prospects, the two young men eventually decide to move on down the street and try their luck at the house with the worst reputation on campus, the Delta Tau

Chi house. As they enter, their welcome is a stark contrast to what they just received. Instead of hostesses in semi-formal dress recruited from one of the sororities, they are greeted by John Belushi's character, Bluto. Toting a glass of such size that one quickly realizes that the beer it bears is better judged by its quantity than its quality, Bluto welcomes them with "Grab a brew! Don't cost nothing." The rush party at the Delta Tau Chi House is anything but orderly. In contrast to their neighbors, the Deltas appear to be doing what they normally do on almost any night of the year—the only change being that prospective pledges are welcome to join them on this particular night.

The rest of the movie follows the experiences of Flounder and Pinto as they become Delta pledges. These experiences include almost anything and everything one can possibly imagine, from smoking marijuana with an underachieving English professor to contemplating sexual intercourse (and arguably sexually assaulting) with the mayor's fifteen-year-old daughter who passed out due to alcohol consumption. One of the members even goes so far as to seduce the wife of the dean of students. These antics lead to the revocation of the Deltas' charter as well as their eventual expulsion from Faber College. Far from allowing their expulsion to be the last chapter in their college careers, the Deltas respond by crashing the annual homecoming parade. Instead of being a time when the spirit of the college comes to a high point for both students and alumni, the Deltas turn the parade into an exercise in utter chaos.

National Lampoon's *Animal House* brings with it a satirical critique of the authoritarian and perhaps overly serious nature of college life in the early 1960s. Released in 1976, college life had come through the upheaval of the late 1960s and early 1970s. The more formal qualities that were willingly accepted by most students in the previous generation were now gone. While I do not advocate a return to the early 1960s, remembering that racial and gender discrimination defined many of these cultures, I am concerned by the way this film blurs the line between fact and fiction in college life. In the end, is life beyond the classroom defined by excess and immorality in any number of forms? For the Christian college, an institution which seeks to encourage each student in the praise and worship of God, the out-of-class experience is not extracurricular. These institutions seek to integrate the in-class experience (or the curricular) and the out-of-class experience (or the co-curricular) under the experience of common worship. Otherwise, the best-case scenario is that students adopt the rationale of work hard (when in class) and play hard (when out of class). The out-of-class experience then comes to be defined by a circus-like host of diversions accentuated by the constant presence of excessive quantities of grain alcohol. The worst-case scenario is an animal house—an experience where any inclination to work is eclipsed by the propensity to play even harder.

Defining the Curricular and the Co-curricular

On most campuses, student life professionals, not faculty members, oversee the co-curricular realm. This group of professionals emerged during the early part of the twentieth century and became common on college campuses during the 1960s. At one time, faculty oversaw areas such as residence halls, student activities, and student government. As faculty retreated further into the classroom, the laboratory, or the studio, however, student life professionals became more numerous and the division between life inside and outside the classroom widened. When a firm distinction separates the curricular and the co-curricular from one another, students adapt to this divided existence. The motivated student may work very hard at her or his academic pursuits but see no relationship between those efforts and other facets of college life. As a result, the propensity to see academic efforts as work also yields the propensity to view other involvements simply as play. Too many colleges and universities allowed this to happen by abandoning what was once known as the *en loco parentis* model of interacting with students. Colleges and universities did not necessarily want to take the place of parents or be the *local parents* for students. But they did accept, particularly the faculty, a significant measure of responsibility for the well-being of their students.

To prove this unfortunate point, simply observe the parking lots serving faculty and staff members on any number of college campuses. If you start your vigil at about 7:30 A.M., you will begin to see the faculty arriving on campus. Their cars will likely stay in those same spaces until about 4:30 P.M. when they slowly start to depart from campus. By 6:00 P.M., those same parking lots will likely look like they did prior to 7:30 A.M. However, on a residential campus, almost all of the students are still there. They live on campus. They take their meals on campus. And, of course, they study on campus. The college experience is about much more than just what a student learns during a particular class period; rather, the experience continues on through the day and into the night (for some nocturnal students, the distinction between day and night becomes difficult to determine). As a result, learning continues in the absence of the faculty. What kind of learning is taking place and who, if anyone, is leading it?

Well-educated student life professionals understand that they are responsible for ordering these co-curricular learning experiences. Students in college certainly need and deserve some "down time" that they can define within certain parameters on their own. However, the larger co-curricular realm needs to be defined by a group of colleagues such as student life professionals who take into account the school's educational mission. These people are trained to understand that just as much learning, if not more, occurs beyond the classroom as inside it. The question then becomes not whether students will learn in the co-curricular arena, but *what* they will learn. Some of the learning experiences designed by student life professionals are as simple as helping students better understand how one gets along with roommates. Others are as complex as learning how a residence hall community works together to serve a group of economically oppressed people living just beyond the college gates. Student life professionals understand that these wide-ranging learning experiences are difficult for one person to address. While faculty members and student life professionals are each responsible for particular arenas of college life, it is ideal for students to see the two groups working together to develop learning experiences designed to meet the needs of the whole student.

Defining the Curricular and the Co-curricular for the Christian College

While the integration of the curricular and the co-curricular is essential to preclude the "work hard, play hard" mentality from infiltrating any college environment, the stakes are even higher in the Christian college environment. As an institution that understands its mission to teach students to offer their whole lives in praise and worship of God, the Christian college cannot relegate faith to any particular dimension of college life such as chapel or religion courses. If anything, faith must be the unifying theme that defines the Christian college experience as a whole. In Western society, faith has often been relegated to emotional, rather than rational, dimensions of life. This tendency creates real challenges for the Christian college. While students are often apt to see faith as a resource for how they are to treat other people, they are equally apt to see faith as secondary to what are deemed more rational or intellectual efforts. In perhaps oversimplified terms, this difference is often summed up by what science is perceived to be able to prove versus what faith is perceived to be able to prove. However, faith is neither emotional nor rational. Instead, it should provide an overarching influence that brings together all of the various and competing influences in our lives.

With this division between the intellectual and emotional, students can easily view their in-class experiences (or the curricular arena) as their public life defined by rationality, and their out-of-class experiences (or the co-curricular arena) as their private life defined by emotion. This is a problem for two reasons. First, this division minimizes the significance of learning that takes place inside the classroom. For example, one cannot understand the full significance of a study of poverty encountered in a sociology class by simply sorting through data. Numbers can possess a tremendous amount of descriptive power. We can learn who is most likely to fall under the poverty level and what circumstances increase a person's statistical chances of facing that challenge. However, in order to truly understand poverty, one must also hear the voices of those who find themselves struggling to be free of its grip. Personal narratives provide a sense of context that escapes the descriptive power of data and demand that students draw on their rational and emotional capacities in a near-integrated sense.

Second, this division minimizes the experiences that students have outside of the classroom. For example, learning to live with a roommate is something a student cannot do by simply drawing upon his or her emotional capacities. Rational thought must be involved, too, but in an integrated manner. Emotional impulses cannot dictate how a student should interact with her or his roommate. Rational efforts such as the construction of a list of pros and cons also often falls short of the goal of truly learning to live together. Both are needed and neither is as distinct from the other as we might initially think.

In the end, the success of co-curricular experiences is measured by their ability to be integrated with the curricular. Such integration minimizes the "work hard, play hard" mentality and precludes a possible slide toward "why work, just party hard all the time" mentality. While the experiences portrayed in *Animal House* are hyperbolic, they capture glimpses of a reality that takes place on too many college campuses today. The integration I am advocating counters this reality. But basic integration is not enough on the Christian college campus. The curricular and the co-curricular are not only integrated but integrated under the larger goal of forming within students the desire to order all of life in pursuit of praise and worship of God.

What Does the Literature Say?

While *Animal House* may be an exaggerated parody of college life, it also reflects some reality. There is plenty of reason to be concerned about the out-of-class activities of many college students. Typically, college students spend a large amount of time involved in activities unrelated to classes. As you may have heard, the tried and true formula is that students should spend at least two hours outside of class reading, studying, and completing assignments for every hour they spend in class. Thus, if the average full-time academic load is fifteen class hours a week, we would expect them to spend another thirty hours studying, doing homework, and preparing for class. The two figures added together equal forty-five hours or roughly the equivalent of a full-time job. Interestingly, according to the results of the 2009 National Survey of Student Engagement (NSSE), a prominent higher educational assessment initiative, 62% of first-year students and 61% of seniors spend fifteen or less hours per week studying. How many students, you might wonder, approach that magic number of thirty hours per week? This initiative showed that only 10% of first-year students and 13% of seniors spend twenty-six or more hours per week studying.[1]

If students are not spending their time studying, it is reasonable to ask just what they are doing outside of the classroom. The answer to this question is complex but well worth our attention. In reality, while students are involved in many educationally purposeful activities, they are also involved in some activities which can be quite destructive. One prominent area of concern, especially for parents who are committed to the spiritual well-being and development of their daughters and sons, is the issue of alcohol abuse. One need only take a quick scan of the statistics related to college student alcohol abuse to get a sense of the enormity of the issue and the devastating consequences. According to the Task Force on College Drinking of the National Advisory Council on Alcohol Abuse and Alcoholism:[2]

- 1,700 college students between the ages of eighteen and twenty-four die each year from alcohol-related unintentional injuries, including motor vehicle crashes;
- 599,000 students between the ages of eighteen and twenty-four are unintentionally injured under the influence of alcohol;
- More than 97,000 students between the ages of eighteen and twenty-four are victims of alcohol-related sexual assault or date rape;
- 400,000 students between the ages of eighteen and twenty-four had unprotected sex and more than 100,000 of them report having been too intoxicated to know if they consented to having sex;
- About twenty-five percent of college students report academic consequences of their drinking including missing class, falling behind, doing poorly on exams or papers, and receiving lower grades overall;
- 2.1 million students between the ages of eighteen and twenty-four drove under the influence of alcohol last year;

- More than twenty-five percent of administrators from schools with relatively low drinking levels and over fifty percent from schools with high drinking levels say their campuses have a "moderate" or "major" problem with alcohol-related property damage; and
- Thirty-one percent of college students met criteria for a diagnosis of alcohol abuse and six percent for a diagnosis of alcohol dependence in the past twelve months, according to questionnaire-based self-reports about their drinking.

The sharing of these facts is not intended to cause alarm or reaction but rather to illustrate the forces that may detract from or even completely derail a student's college experience. These figures represent untold amounts of wasted time, lost money, shattered dreams, and unreached potential. However, the real point intended here is that what college students do matters. Put another way, the manner in which a college structures, values, and supports the out-of-class experience of its students has a tremendous impact on their learning, lives, and experiences.

Given the statistics on alcohol abuse, it might be tempting to jump to the conclusion that when students are not in class or studying, they are partying. However, this conclusion would be wrong. Students actually do report involvement in a number of other very positive activities, including spending time with friends, exercising, volunteering, working for pay, and participating in groups and clubs. These activities lead us to ask, "What about the other curriculum? More specifically, what are students experiencing and how are they learning and growing as a result of their out-of-class involvement?

For any institution to be successful in delivering a quality education, strong emphasis must be placed on out-of-class experiences. For Christian institutions, the understanding that all of life affords an opportunity for learning, growth, and development is foundational. Christian educators more than all others should understand "whole-person education" and recognize the powerful opportunity they have to influence hearts, minds, and lives. Higher education practitioners realize how vital extracurricular opportunities are for significant growth, learning, and development to take place. The recognition of the importance of this realm has led educators to label it "the other curriculum."[3] The best educational experience is one that connects what happens in the classroom with what happens outside of it, an idea known as "the seamless curriculum."

While this may sound good, everything, including the extra-curricular (or, more accurately, co-curricular), must have an explicit educational purpose for it to happen. If you want to know how much a particular college or university really believes this and how intentional they will be in maximizing the benefits of the out-of-class experience, ask them for their student life curriculum. If it does not exist, it is highly unlikely that they are committed to or prepared for accomplishing the good things to which they may give lip service or even genuinely aspire. An institution without an academic curriculum would lose its accreditation. In the same way, one without a student life curriculum cannot be seen as seriously trying to accomplish educational ends outside of the classroom. As the social critic Neil Postman reminds us, "to become a better person because of something you have learned—to appropriate an insight, a concept, a vision, so that your world is altered . . . you need a reason. . . . For school to make sense, the young, their parents, and their teachers must have a god to serve, or even better, several gods. If they have none, school is pointless."[4] And, I might add, so are students' out-of-class activities.

Noted higher education scholar George Kuh has studied the out-of-class experiences of students extensively and found that students overwhelmingly acknowledged great personal growth and development as a result of their extra-curricular involvement.[5] Kuh characterizes these out-of-class experiences as a "real world laboratory" where students are able to apply and further understand what they are learning inside the classroom.[6] Many students believe that their greatest learning occurs in those experiences. While this perspective can surely be argued, what cannot be argued is the incredible educational potential that exists when these two realms are brought together.

As you will remember from our discussion of Alexander Astin's "involvement theory" in chapter two, students learn best in situations in which they invest both time and emotional energy. The emotional energy is the result of an activity whose purpose is clear and compelling from the student's perspective. This simple truth has important implications for "the way we do education." In order for students to truly learn, they must perceive that educational activities are relevant to what they value. Oftentimes, it is the experiential nature of co-curricular activities that help students to make these connections. At the best Christian colleges, co-curricular experiences are designed to highlight, illustrate, supplement, and give opportunity to interact meaningfully with the curricular in order to foster positive learning and development.

Perhaps the most common out-of-class activity for students is living in a residence hall. While "dorm life" is often thought to be simply a necessity required because students need a place to stay while they take classes, such a view misses the incredible educational potential that exists in these settings. Residence halls are a common feature of virtually all traditional Christian institutions, so it is very likely that your daughter or son will be living in one. If she or he decides to attend a local Christian college, you may be tempted to save money by having her or him live at home. Let me strongly encourage you to consider otherwise, lest one of the most important learning experiences available to college students be missed. Beyond the benefits of learning to live away from home, learning to live with people different from oneself, and learning to work out conflicts with others, there are additional advantages to be gained.

Given the amount of time students spend in their residence halls, these living-learning communities arguably have the greatest potential for changing students. Noted higher education scholars Ernest Pascarella and Patrick Terenzini call living on campus the most significant "determinant of impact."[7] Their work indicates that the greatest benefits are obtained from the residential programs that work hardest to connect the academic and social experiences of the students. It makes sense that students benefit when they are taught to make connections between the different pieces of their college experience. Similarly, they learn best when their learning is not compartmentalized but, rather, reinforced from a variety of directions. Studies have linked living in a residence hall with gains in "aesthetic, cultural, and intellectual values; liberalizing of social, political, and religious values and attitudes; development of more positive self-concepts, intellectual orientation, autonomy, and independence; tolerance, empathy, and the ability to relate to others; . . . the use of principled reasoning to judge moral issues . . . [and] the likelihood of persisting in college and earning a bachelor's degree."[8] Needless to say, this list contains some very important benefits. If some of the items give you pause, consider that these studies reflect a wide variety of types of institutions and that the content of the "other curriculum" and its impact at a given institution will be dictated by that institution's mission.

As important as these benefits are, merely living in a residence hall may not be enough. One study found that it was the students who were most highly involved in their residence halls who were most pleased with their college community academically and socially. Consequently, these students found it "easier to study and collaborate academically with others in their community."[9] Additionally, residence hall involvement was found to be helpful in modeling healthy community involvement for students later in life, a result that is closely aligned with the goal of most colleges: to produce students who are motivated and prepared to be civically engaged. Even more importantly, students who are willing and able to be involved in their communities will be much better able to be "salt and light" in their local neighborhood as well as effective participants and leaders in the local church.

Almost every college offers the promise of preparing leaders. Somewhere in the literature of most schools is a catchy tagline to the effect of: "Ajax University, preparing tomorrow's leaders today." While this may be good advertising, it is also a noble goal and one that is consistent with the historical aims of higher education. One of the original and longest-standing purposes of American higher education has been to prepare civic, educational, church, and business leaders. Thus, Christian institutions arguably understand the need to provide student leadership training and opportunities. Student leadership positions such as student government officer, resident assistant in a residence hall, or leader of a student club or service group provide tremendous experiences and learning opportunities. Such opportunities are critical and beneficial for the "private good" (the individual), the "public good" (the community and the country), and the "Kingdom good" (the body of believers). Research supports the benefits that students receive as a result of participation in leadership activities, and students clearly note the impact that these experiences have on their personal development.[10]

A review of the personal benefits gained through participation in leadership activities is impressive. Among the outcomes are conflict resolution skills, the ability to set goals, decision-making ability, a sense of personal ethics, and commitment to civic responsibility. All of these are outcomes that ought to be of interest to those with a concern for college students, the nation, and the church.[11] Other research tells us that participation in student leadership influences students well beyond graduation. Alumni often acknowledge that personal and professional success in the present is due to student leadership involvement during college. Student leadership programs not only provide a platform to meet people of all types, but also foster management and teamwork skills. When referring to current jobs, alumni point to past leadership experiences as central in improving interpersonal communication skills, professional poise, and confidence.[12]

Christian colleges understand that one of their primary roles is to prepare students to serve. While some types of institutions market themselves simply as a means of improving one's opportunities for greater earning and influence, Christian education has a markedly different end. While Christian colleges certainly understand that their graduates will be eligible for the same kinds of material benefits afforded the graduates of other kinds of institutions, producing such gains is not the purpose for which they exist. Furthermore, they try to help their students to understand that sacrificing some of these benefits may even be part of Christ's calling on their lives. This being the case, Christian colleges work hard to assure that students understand the central place of service in the gospel message and to prepare them to serve effectively in whatever roles they are called.

One of the most productive means of doing this is through what are called "service-learning opportunities." Service-learning is a relatively recent development and thus this phrase may be unfamiliar to many. It is defined as an "organized service activity that meets identified community needs and [obliges students to] reflect on the service activity in such a way as to gain further understanding of course content."[13] This connection of actual service with the classroom experience has proven to be an amazingly effective teaching strategy. The service-learning movement is a major force in higher education today because of its recognized power as a teaching tool and its use as a vehicle for accomplishing the broader mission of higher education—to serve the greater good. Through service-learning activities, students connect in-class learning with hands-on work within the local community or in more distant locations. Among the benefits gained from these courses are a better grasp of the discipline being studied, a heightened sense of civic responsibility, and enhanced reflective abilities.[14]

In one study of service-learning programs, students in a political science course were put in two groups: the first with a service-learning component and the second without. While the classroom experience of both groups was identical, the students who participated in the service component received far more benefit in the development of their personal values, their inclination toward a community connection, and the academic learning that they experienced in the course.[15]

I could go on and on, giving evidence of the benefits of the-out-of class experience. For our purposes, however, these examples will suffice. The research is conclusive: what happens out of class is important, and it is a major enhancement to a student's educational experience. While some of the experiences of college life are no doubt frivolous, the weight of the evidence clearly indicates that students' involvement in purposeful activities, from hallway conversations about world events to extensive service and leadership experiences, will benefit them in the classroom, in the workplace, and in life beyond college. Thoughtful parents will work hard to help their daughters and sons capture all of the potential benefits of the college experience by encouraging them to invest themselves in these pursuits.

What Can Parents Do?

You may be asking yourself as a parent whether this discussion on *Animal House*-like behavior is pertinent to the Christian college. After all, aren't Christian colleges providing safe and nurturing environments where students' spiritual as well as academic growth is fostered, and where they are shielded from the influences found on many college campuses as depicted by the mythical Faber College? The answer to the first part of this question is an unqualified "yes" while the answer to the second part is not answered so easily. Every Christian college I am familiar with has in place policies and practices that prohibit and limit behaviors associated with the hedonistic depiction of American college campus life found at Faber. However, the implementation of these policies and practices does not erect a magical "bubble" impenetrable by the problematic issues such as binge drinking, promiscuous sexual behavior, and illegal drug usage that plague the average college campus. All of the issues that the average campus faces are also present on Christian college campuses, although the degrees, frequency, and visibility likely differ. This is fundamental to the process of choosing a Christian college. Is their purpose to protect and shelter students from the issues in our culture or is it to prepare them to be positive change agents in a world that needs moral Christians applying biblical principles to these issues? Obviously the latter fits with the scriptural mandates to "be in the world but not of it" and to "no longer be conformed to this world but be transformed by the renewing of your minds" (Romans 12:2).

What is and should be markedly different is how a Christian college responds to these issues. Take, for instance, underage drinking—on most public campuses, a common approach is to encourage responsible drinking and to provide programming that educates students on the danger of binge drinking and driving while intoxicated. The Christian campus may address responsible drinking but also introduce the importance of aspects such as faith, integrity, and community responsibility in helping students consider the role alcohol plays in society, church, and their individual lives as Christians. Again, the same issue but a markedly different response. One is focused on the bottom line of avoiding problems or "staying out of trouble," while the other approaches the issue from a stewardship perspective.

Students and parents would do well to acknowledge that the Christian college does not provide immunity from the "evils of the world" and that it will take discernment and wise decision making to thrive at a Christian school. There are two specific myths or misconceptions that parents and students should understand while considering collegiate behavior as depicted at Faber College and how it relates to the Christian college experience. The first is the myth that "sowing one's wild oats" is a natural and almost necessary rite of passage for college students regardless of what type of school they attend. The second myth is the previously mentioned separation that exists between the in-class and out-of-class experiences. This myth holds to the notion that the classroom or academic side is where learning takes place and is, therefore, the "workplace" of college life and that the out-of-class experience is where the fun part of campus life takes place and seldom the two shall meet.

The first myth is an extension of the "boys will be boys" mentality and the notion that the four years of college are a time of experimentation and a part of the natural maturation process. The sense is that if I don't experience it, I cannot really tell if it is right or wrong. This view is problematic for a host of reasons, possibly the most primary being that it reflects the mindset that the individual is the primary source of truth and morality. This view ignores the fact that in a Christian understanding of reality, the Bible provides the ultimate source of authority and guidance. Predictably, this kind of thinking and decision-making can lead to a number of problematic lifestyle issues. This mindset results in students who view their time in college, even at a Christian college, as a "gap experience"—in other words, a time where they put their personal and spiritual development on hold until graduation. This has potentially devastating implications, such as the stunting of spiritual growth and the development of attitudes and habits inconsistent with productive and faithful discipleship.

I am not implying that life at a Christian college should not be fun or even exhilarating. I found my own experience at a Christian college so compelling that I basically never left and have spent my entire adult life in this environment. It is and should be an incredibly invigorating experience. Far from being dull and mundane, your daughter or son's experience at a Christian college should be vibrant, fun, and ultimately fulfilling. However, it is important to recognize the difference between engagement in an exhilarating journey of exploring God's creation and learning how to present ourselves as living sacrifices (Romans 12) versus engaging in the pursuit of folly. "Folly" as described in Proverbs (5:21-23) leads to separation from God, while the journey toward presenting oneself in worship leads to relationship with God.

Please allow me to illustrate the difference between these two approaches. First, consider the experiences of Carl, a fictitious student, who finds himself expelled from a Christian college after several disciplinary hearings for behaviors ranging from alcohol consumption, academic dishonesty, sexual misconduct, and finally, smoking marijuana. Throughout his disciplinary meetings, Carl asserts that he was only trying to have a little fun; after all, isn't that what college is for? Compare Carl to Ed, who has also sought out fun activities during his college career, such as playing intramural sports, participating in spring break mission trips, studying abroad for a semester, involvement in campus organizations, and pursuing a healthy social life. Both Carl and Ed have "had fun" during their college experiences, but Ed's pursuits have helped him present his mind and body as sacrifices of worship while Carl has pursued folly. These characters are fictitious but realistic portrayals of scenarios occurring on Christian college campuses every day. Carl's story is not meant to represent "bad" students but rather to serve as an example of how some students can waste a valuable opportunity by giving into the myth that college is a place to sow wild oats instead of a time to pursue meaningful personal and spiritual development.

Now let's address the second myth, the artificial separation between the classroom and the rest of the collegiate experience. Again, this myth perpetuates the thought that the only true learning that occurs at college is in the classroom. To be sure, the classroom is essential to the learning process, and in a traditional liberal arts institution, it is the key element. However, as noted earlier, higher education research has shown over the past three to four decades that the co-curricular or out-of-class experiences provide rich opportunities for learning and integrating classroom teaching into real-world settings.[16] In the 1980s and 1990s, educators began to focus on the importance of the out-of-class experiences, leading to the "learner centered" approach to higher education. This has led to "seamless learning"[17] initiatives to integrate both in- and out-of-classroom experiences in a holistic approach to higher education. This approach discourages the mindset that academics (the classroom) are the work side of college while everything else is the play.

This is particularly true for a Christian institution, which focuses on stewardship in order to help students grow spiritually, intellectually, and emotionally. Its ultimate goal is to teach students to present themselves, body and spirit, in worship and service to God. This makes it uniquely valuable in the world of higher education. If a Christian college is not providing this component, one can reasonably ask how they are different from their secular counterparts and how they justify typically higher tuition rates. Even if a Christian college is fulfilling its purpose, it is possible for a student to attend and not take advantage of the opportunities. Therefore, it is imperative that students not neglect the wonderful opportunities for learning and spiritual growth available in the co-curricular offerings at a Christian college.

So, how can you as a parent both help your son navigate the process of choosing a Christian college and encourage him to make the most of his experience? The place to start is an examination of the motives for attending a Christian college. Are you choosing a Christian school because it is the ideal environment for him to learn and grow, or are you sending him there so he will be sheltered from the problems of large, public institutions? In other words, are you sending him to a "bubble" in order to shield him from the world or to a training ground that will nurture an understanding of biblical principles for dealing with real life and real world problems? Is this your choice or is this your son's choice of a college? Is he committed to attending a Christian school, or is he only making this choice due to your influence? It is vitally important to your son's educational experience that he owns the decision to attend a Christian college. Students who attend a Christian college to appease their parents rather than to fulfill their own goals can have difficult adjustments to these campuses. You can guide and encourage, but, in the end, the decision needs to be his.

Once you have finished this self-examination, I have two specific recommendations for parents. The first is to develop realistic expectations of the college by thoroughly researching the institutional policies that will shape your son's college experience. Specifically, you should look for lifestyle expectations and related policies that will give you a good indication of how the college views its role in shaping behaviors. As stated earlier, every Christian college will have policies that address behavioral issues, but these policies and the motivations for them differ between colleges. One way to assess this is to examine a school's discipline policies and procedures. At one end of the continuum, you will find schools that are more redemptive in nature and, at the other end, schools that are more accountability oriented in nature. The continuum at Christian colleges is going to span the gap between a traditional view of the college as *en loco parentis* to a more contemporary view of college as *en loco amice* (a wise uncle or mentor).[18] The majority of Christian colleges fall somewhere between these two extremes and will have both redemptive and accountability-oriented elements in their disciplinary processes. These policies and how they are implemented can give insight into what you can expect from the college.

You should also find out what issues are present on campus. There are two venues for this information. First, a discussion with the dean of students or another student affairs staff member can provide valuable information and insight into the campus climate. Second, campuses receiving federal financial aid are required to produce an annual crime report, showing the number and type of crimes committed on campus each year. This information will help you develop realistic expectations of both your son and the college, which will guide you as you support him.

The second recommendation for parents is to develop a healthy balance of support and freedom in your involvement in your son's educational experiences. The key is to stay engaged to the point that you provide support and encouragement but not so overly involved that you stifle his ability to develop independently. This is one of the most courageous steps we can take as parents. It does not mean abdicating our roles by just releasing our daughters and sons into the world to find their way, but it does mean we need to give them the freedom to explore God's calling for their lives. It is finding the right balance between support and challenge that allows them to mature into the woman or man God intends them to be. We want them to be ready to follow God's will for their lives, and this will likely mean encouraging them to step out of their (and, likely, our own) comfort zones as they go through the refining process. The Christian college has many opportunities and partnerships for both your son and you in this process.

Conclusion

Separation of the curricular and the co-curricular realms of college life can prove to be a destructive reality to any college or university. While the images found in *Animal House* are exaggerated, they do exist in different forms on many campuses, and even Christian colleges and universities can face these challenges. An important part of the solution is to connect the curricular and the co-curricular as much as possible in order to show your child how to integrate what they think with what they do. As parents, you play a key role in helping your daughters and sons not only to get involved on campus but also to get involved for the right reasons. While the Christian college is a place where fun is a large part of the experience, it must also help its students to rethink their definitions of fun and fulfillment in the light of our larger calling to offer praise and worship to God.

PART II

THE SEASONS OF COLLEGE LIFE

When the Only Thing to Fear Is Fear Itself

Lessons from the First Year

Perhaps a worthy rival to *Animal House* is *Revenge of the Nerds*. While film critics may argue that *Animal House* exceeds *Revenge of the Nerds* in relation to any set of cinematic standards, *Revenge of the Nerds* did spawn three sequels to *Animal House*'s none. Set at Adams College (filmed at the University of Arizona), *Revenge of the Nerds* follows the trials that befall two first-year students seeking to find their way. In fact, the plot for the film is basically defined by the constant search of these two students, Gilbert and Louis, and their other fellow "nerds" to find a home away from home.

The movie begins when a stunt during a party at the Alpha Beta fraternity house goes awry, burning the house to the ground. Populated by football players, the Alpha Betas possess the mindset that the Adams campus is theirs to control. When they need a place to live, they descend upon a group of first-year students and throw them out of their home. Unwilling to stand up for these now-homeless students, the university provides them with accommodations in the gymnasium. At one point, only a mesh screen separates these sleeping students from what appears to be a physical education class. Eventually, even these relatively hapless students become frustrated with their surroundings. They band together and decide that together they are going to find a new home.

In true 1980s fashion (the film was released in 1984), this band of brothers represents an array of all-too-familiar typecasts. Gilbert and Lewis are your quintessential nerds—pants pulled up too high, pocket protectors, horned rimmed glasses, and so on. Comparable in appearance, yet lacking any of the social qualities possessed by Gilbert and Lewis, is Arnold Poindexter. There is a foreign exchange student, Takashi. Lamar Latrell is the shamelessly feminine member of the group. Harold Wormser is the boy genius and Duddly "Booger" Dawson is as unhygienic as he is crass. What they lack in social capital at Adams, they possess in brains and creativity. They not only transform a dilapidated home worthy of being condemned into the nicest residence on campus, but they decide to form the Adams chapter of Lambda Lambda Lambda.

Despite their success, Gilbert, Louis, and the rest of the Tri-Lams continue to be persecuted by the Alpha Betas. They realize that the only way to be accepted is to seize control of the Greek Council. Long controlled by groups such as the Alpha Betas, leadership of the Greek Council goes to the winner of the Greek Games—an assortment of endeavors consisting of well-defined games of skill such as a belching contest and drunken tricycle race. Although down early, the Tri-Lams bounce back, capitalizing on their creativity, and are declared the winners. The movie closes with an emotion-filled scene where a host of individuals declare they are either nerds or that they are in love with nerds. By sheer force of will, Gilbert, Louis, and the rest of the Tri-Lams eventually find a home at Adams College.

Beyond the problems with its dazzling array of stereotypes, *Revenge of the Nerds* creates the recurring impression that the way we welcome people into a new educational community is through hazing or even torment. The concept of the initiation ritual is not one defined by grace and empathy. In contrast, it is defined by derision and humiliation. Fraternities, sororities, residence halls, athletic teams, and a vast array of clubs have confused the welcoming of the newest members of their communities with hosts of unfortunate words and deeds. Persistence through the hazing, similar to the force of will exhibited by Gilbert, Louis, and the rest of the Tri-Lams, is what wins one a place in one's new home. Most college administrators would be horrified to think that the welcome the Tri-Lambdas received was anything like reality at their institution. Many administrators at secular colleges and universities have worked tirelessly to eliminate such forms of treatment of first-year students. For the Christian college administrator, however, the responsibility is even greater. Aspiring to form within students the desire to order all of life in the pursuit of offering praise and worship to God, the Christian college must initiate new members into its community through the practice of Christian hospitality.

The Offering of Hospitality to First-Year Students

To administrators at secular colleges and universities, the treatment offered to first-year students is to be defined by tolerance. Each student, regardless of whether she or he is a "nerd" or not, possesses certain rights. Other students are expected to respect these rights and not to impede the pursuits of any of the newest members of their communities. While an admirable beginning, the practice of tolerance is not enough within the

Christian college environment. The underlying problem is that the standard of tolerance still allows for the understanding that our individual well-being is separate and distinct from the well-being of others. Each person is sovereign and all we owe one another is to not hinder each other's efforts. While reaching out to one another is preferable, the practice of tolerance does not in any way bind one to reach out to the other.

While the Christian college campus is also called to be a place that practices tolerance and respect, such a community is also bound to practice hospitality. The difference here is that the practice of Christian hospitality begins with the assumption that our well-being is inextricably bound to the well-being of others. This understanding is the logical extension of countless biblical injunctions. The Apostle Paul reminds us that we are to love others as Christ loved us. He sums up such an understanding with the admonishment to practice hospitality. "Love must be sincere. Hate what is evil; cling to what is good. Be devoted to one another in brotherly love. Honor one another above yourselves. Never be lacking in zeal, but keep your spiritual fervor, serving the Lord. Be joyful in hope, patient in affliction, faithful in prayer. Share with God's people who are in need. Practice hospitality" (Romans 12:9-13).

For the Apostle Paul, hospitality proves to be a defining practice of Christian love. As members of Christ's body, we are called to share in the joy and bear the burdens of others. Kim Phipps, President of Messiah College, once remarked that hospitality is essential to Christian communities, particularly Christian academic communities, because "community is the acknowledgement of our unavoidable interrelatedness; it is the admission that we are dependent upon each other."[1]

If Scriptural injunctions lead us in this direction, the very nature of our worship together is designed to refine this understanding. In baptism, we welcome new members into the body of Christ. Some Christian traditions go so far as to describe baptism as being akin to grafting a previously disparate branch into a new tree. People who were once alienated from us become our brothers and sisters in Christ. The practice of the Lord's Supper reinforces this same lesson. When we eat of Christ's body and drink of Christ's blood, we are reminded that our existence is not determined by our own individual efforts but is sustained by Christ as members of his body. Common worship, as practiced within the context of the Christian college, defines the community we share in common and stands as a reminder of the true source of our identity.

Offering Hospitality: An Example

In comparison to the welcome that Louis, Gilbert, and the rest of the Tri-Lams received at Adams College, I was once privileged to witness the power that hospitality can offer to a first-year student and her mother at a Christian college. I will just warn you that the day set aside for first-year students to move into their residence halls is chaotic by its very nature. We can do everything in our power to devise efficient traffic patterns, provide clear and concise communication, and offer assistance with unloading, and things may still conjure a visual image of a tsunami of personal possessions washing upon the shore of the campus. The reality is that moving that many students, most of whom have never met one another, into a common space just takes time. In addition to time, however, it takes hospitality. Parents rightfully deserve to be assured on that emotional day that their daughters and sons have decided to join a community that welcomes them with nothing less than the qualities of biblically mandated hospitality.

We were fortunate enough that day to avoid the rain. Faculty members and fellow administrators from across the campus had come to welcome our new students and their parents. For their troubles, we were kind enough to offer these volunteers complimentary orientation t-shirts. Our provost, new to the campus that year, was an insightful administrator as well as arguably the world's leading scholar in his field. His good intentions, however, did fall a little short when it came to fashion. He had donned the orientation t-shirt and a pair of cargo shorts. However, he forgot (or so we assumed) to bring a pair of athletic shoes. As a result, his dark socks and loafers spoke something all too loudly about the fashion sense we academics often possess. He quickly met the first car, greeted a mother and her daughter, and then proceeded to help them carry their things up to a room on the third floor.

After approximately a dozen trips up and down the stairs in the summer heat, the mother decided to ask our provost what he did at the college. Up to that point the mother and daughter had simply known him as Don—the name written on his nametag. Don hesitated for a moment and then shared with this mother and her daughter that he was the provost. The mother was not sure how to respond. She was a little taken aback by the fact that the chief academic officer for the college had just carried her daughter's things up to her room. Mom was anxious about the decision that her daughter had made. I later discovered that this student was the first in her family to go to college and was the only child raised by this single mom.

By practicing hospitality, however, Don had communicated to this mother that her daughter's presence at the college was appreciated. While the college would not try to replace her role as a parent, Don's actions communicated to this mom that her daughter was now also part of an extended family. Although this transition would come with its challenges, her daughter had found a home away from the only home she had known.

Receiving Hospitality

In order for this home away from home to be found, not only must the Christian college practice hospitality, but first-year students must be prepared to accept it. The key to making a successful transition to college is a student's ability to integrate into a community. Some students get too involved and forsake critical matters of self-care such as sleep and a balanced diet—some students become nocturnal to the point that they even come to think of the first meal of the day as lunch. Other students get involved in the wrong activities—alcohol and drugs are critical public health concerns on any campus. Parents can play a crucial role in helping their daughters and sons make wise choices about when, where, and how to get involved on campus, recognizing that the receipt of hospitality is critical to success at a Christian college. The following section offers some insights as to how parents can help their daughters and sons find a home away from home.

What Does the Literature Say?

For most students, moving away from home to live in a building full of strangers with an unfamiliar, perhaps intimidating roommate is among the most frightening prospects of early adulthood. And parents, please let me remind you, I am talking about your daughters and sons, not you.

While the challenges that come with starting college are many and varied, I have found that unquestionably the greatest and most anxiety producing of them all is the fear of living with a roommate. If we could somehow wave a magic wand that would guarantee first-year students that their roommate would be a loyal, thoughtful, fun, and supportive friend, their other fears about beginning college would quickly fade away.

The social networks that incoming first-year students have built throughout their entire lives at home are suddenly gone, and they are faced with having to foster new relationships, navigate a new, less nurturing and more competitive educational environment, and cope with being away from family and friends. Of course, we cannot forget that many students anticipate the start of their college experience with a great deal of excitement. But the excitement is generally coupled with a fear of the unknown and fears about their ability to fit in and to be successful. Rather than allaying these fears, arrival on campus often accentuates them when new students are surrounded by others who may have more talent, more experience, and more preparation than they do. And even if, as is often the case, the perception is worse than the reality, convincing a novice student of this may be impossible.

Often for the first time, first-year students are expected to function on their own as they navigate their new surroundings and the daily challenges that come with the transition to their new home. Additionally, they have to deal with the emotional ramifications of leaving family and figuring out just what this transition means to their future.

If it is true that today's students come without a strong history of functioning on their own, it may be even more true of students coming to Christian colleges and universities than students attending other types of institutions. Given the strong and appropriate evangelical emphasis on parental involvement, many Christian teens have not had as many opportunities as their secular friends to "test their wings" or to take responsibility for themselves. It is likely that nurturing and well-meaning parents have monitored their children too closely at times, hovering nearby to remind them of their responsibilities and to make sure they are eating properly, sleeping enough, and getting to church and youth group. Although these interventions may have been conducted with great care, thoughtfulness, and concern, they also may have kept the students from getting the trial-and-error practice needed to develop the confidence that they, in fact, are equipped to function on their own.

Oftentimes, as Christian parents, we struggle with knowing how to give our daughters and sons progressively more freedom and responsibility so that they become better and better prepared to function as responsible adults. Because of this, we may be over-involved, or perhaps better said, wrongly involved in their lives. There are many benefits to this involvement; of course, we know that it may protect them from many harmful and even heartbreaking experiences. However, it is also possible to be too engaged and to provide too much direction. The line is often very hard to discern. Even when we do back off enough to let them make their own decisions or take the lead in their lives, we often make the equally damaging mistake of protecting them from the consequences of their actions. In other words, we let them make their own choices but if those choices turn out badly, we step in and "fix" things for them, sending the message that we really do not think that they are capable of resolving the situation on their own. These actions result in young adults who are unable to take responsibility for themselves. As hard as it may be, we have to learn how best to support, encourage, and nurture our daughters and sons without living their lives for them.

Let's consider several of the other opportunities and challenges that face our daughters and sons as they enter college, some of the most important of which are basic life skills. Maintaining mental health, dealing with homesickness, managing time, healthy eating, and developing good sleep patterns are just a few examples of the responsibilities students must begin to handle on their own. Thankfully, colleges that are focused on Christian, whole-person education understand that these are areas of challenge to which they also must give attention. While these colleges will not "babysit" your daughters or sons, most of them will give attention to these matters through campus programs, counseling services, health and nutritional education, and a generally nurturing, supportive environment. The strong sense of community that exists on most of these campuses is a tremendous asset. An environment built upon a Christian worldview and where people are encouraged to be accountable to and for one another can have a remarkable impact on students' growth and maturity. Higher education research has repeatedly shown that the strongest influencers of college students are other college students.[2] This simple concept is an incredibly powerful idea that basically acknowledges and tries to work with the fact that students educate students. And, because this is true, the characteristics, quality, and focus of students attending should be a very important part of choosing a particular college or university. Think "big picture" here. I am not talking about your son's annoying roommate—this is part of life that he needs to learn to deal with; I am talking about the overall quality of the student body. In short, the students who sit alongside your daughters and sons in classes, residence hall discussions, chapel, campus activities, service trips, and Bible studies will have a major impact on what they learn over the next four years.

Nancy Schlossberg, the president of the consulting firm Transition Works, has done extensive research on life transitions and particularly the things that make a transition a positive experience. Her "transition theory" considers both the importance and the challenge of adjusting to major life changes. Her definition of a transition is "any event, or non-event, that results in changed relationships, routines, assumptions, and roles."[3] Of course, leaving home and beginning college certainly qualifies as a major life change. In particular, Schlossberg points to the individual and environmental characteristics that affect the impact a transition will have on a person.

Christian colleges are generally dedicated to ensuring that students grow intellectually, socially, and spiritually; however, the formula for success is complicated. While we expect the college transition to be a positive, growth-producing one, we must heed Schlossberg's warning that transitions "may lead to growth, but decline is also a possible outcome."[4] According to her, the four factors that figure most prominently in students' readiness to cope effectively with a transition are the situation, self, support, and strategies. *Situation* refers to the conditions that a person will encounter in their new circumstances, while *self* relates to the individual characteristics, resilience, and personal resources a person possesses. As you might gather, *support* speaks to the network of resources, human and otherwise, available to a student, and finally, *strategies* indicate one's ability to develop and implement plans to address a situation successfully. In short, the problem-solving, decision-making, and coping skills that your daughter or son developed throughout the formative years will have a direct impact on the ability to make a smooth transition to college.

Similarly, the support your child receives from friends and family at home, a college roommate, and through staff and programs put together by the college will directly impact her or his transition. As you help your daughter or son evaluate colleges, it is necessary to consider the institutions' attitude toward the care and nurture of their students as well as the quality of programs and services designed to help students adjust to college life.

Space prevents us from covering all of the important topics that should be considered, but four examples can illustrate these issues: mental health, homesickness, sleep, and nutrition.

The stress brought on by the transition to this strange, new world can lead to mental health struggles. In particular, parents and colleges must be aware of the increased potential for depression during the transition to college. Richard Kadison, chief of the Mental Health Service at Harvard University, explains that "despite this appearance of comfortable status, secure environment, and a pleasant social world, a multitude of hidden problems have caused a steady and alarming rise in the severity of students' mental health problems."[5] His comment is based on the results of the 2002 American College Health

Association survey which found that 44.7% of all students had "felt so depressed that it was difficult to function at least one time within the last school year."[6] Other studies have shown similar results. This survey represents all types of American colleges and although the results for Christian colleges would likely look somewhat different, students at such institutions are certainly not immune from these problems. Thus, the services and attention given to student mental health are an important part of the educational process.

If students are not emotionally healthy, they simply will not make a healthy adjustment to college. The college years are so critical in students' identity development that helping them to deal constructively with emotional, social, and psychological challenges, both new and ongoing, is an extremely important element of their preparation for living healthy, whole, and successful lives during and after college. Again, how seriously a college takes its responsibility for students' mental health will directly affect their experience and, ultimately, the education they receive. This includes fostering a nurturing, caring, and challenging community and providing vital staffing, services, and programs needed to address these needs. The first year of college will be filled with many wonderful experiences, but students typically go through periods of struggle. Being attentive to mental health needs is critical for both Christian colleges and parents.

For the vast majority of students, the first year also marks their first extended stay away from home. It is not surprising, then, that first-year students often deal with periods of homesickness. One study indicated that 68.8% of first-year students reported experiencing homesickness during their first semester. Of those students, 41% said that this was the first time they had felt homesick. While for most the homesickness lasted only about a week, for almost one in five (18.2%), homesickness persisted for more than eight weeks.[7] Clearly a student dealing with homesickness for one-half to two-thirds of the first semester is unable to engage fully in the community, unlikely to achieve to the best of her or his ability, and unlikely to gain the other non-classroom benefits that are part of the college experience. Worse, such students are prime candidates for academic failure and for dropping out of college.

Social anxiety and the amount of social support a student has are proven influences on homesickness. The more anxiety a student experiences, or the thinner the social support, the greater the likelihood of homesickness.[8] Because the newness of the first-year experience produces especially high levels of anxiety, and since one's campus social support is new and thus underdeveloped, it is understandable that so many first-year students struggle with homesickness. The good news is that, as students adjust to college, initial levels of social anxiety decrease. As a result, homesickness was not related to social anxiety later in the semester.[9] In essence, this research confirms what common sense might suggest: that once students establish relationships at college, homesickness becomes far less of a problem. The practices of hospitality, support, and care that are part of a Christian belief system often translate into efforts to welcome and nurture new students on Christian college campuses, and these efforts make a big difference.

Upon arriving on campus, students, often for the first time, are given the freedom to make their own decisions regarding when to go to bed and when to get up. Unfortunately, many learn by trial and error that the rhythms of the residence hall do not serve them well in trying to develop healthy sleep habits. Though it may seem elementary, understanding the importance of good sleep is crucial to healthy living. Living with a roommate, dealing with the stresses of adjusting to new surroundings, and being immersed in the late-night culture common to college residence halls make positive sleep choices more difficult. Studies confirm that students often struggle in this area. One study found that only 11% of students who completed the Sleep Quality Index (SQI) experienced good sleep quality. Furthermore, the SQI indicated that 73% of students had occasional sleep problems and 15% were classified as poor sleepers. Students indicated that their average bedtime during the week was 11:40 P.M. while during the weekend bedtimes averaged 1:17 A.M. This inconsistency in sleep schedule fosters many of the sleeping problems on college campuses and, of course, can be closely related to a variety of social, emotional, and academic problems.[10]

Without question, college sleep patterns are inconsistent and the discrepancy between weekday and weekend bedtimes and rise times makes it difficult for bodies to find a healthy routine. Even when students make good choices about sleeping, there are often other factors that make it difficult to follow through on these commitments. For instance, a roommate with a very different schedule or different sleep habits as well as noise from activities going on in the hallway may make it difficult to get to sleep at a reasonable time. Forty one percent of students cited noise from others as the primary reason they woke up during the night, illustrating the detrimental results of college culture on quality sleep.[11]

While many first-year students will make bad choices in this regard, they must be given the opportunity to order this aspect of their lives on their own. Schools or parents who interfere in this choice are taking away a key responsibility of young adulthood. Simply put, if students are not ready to decide for themselves when they will go to bed and when they will get up, they are not ready for college. As a residence hall director many years ago, I talked to numerous parents asking about daughters and sons who were not getting enough sleep or who were having a hard time getting up in the morning. One parent went as far as asking me if I could (in a residence hall of three hundred men) wake her son up in the morning because he was having a tough time getting up for his 8:00 A.M. class. I respectfully told her that while I would be happy to talk to her son about healthy habits and choices and the importance of attending class, it would be detrimental to his progress toward adulthood for me to take on this responsibility. While Christian educators understand the important role of boundaries, the school that allows as much freedom as is reasonable and healthy is the school that ultimately has the best opportunity to guide its students toward a healthy and responsible lifestyle.

Like sleeping, eating habits may seem pretty elementary when considering the key issues with which first-year students must contend. However, the importance of learning to make healthy eating choices independently is also crucial to an optimal adjustment to college. The phrase "freshman 15" (referring to pounds of weight gained) is well known for a reason; many first-year students struggle to make healthy eating choices, especially during their first year. Studies have shown that weight gain during college is a reality. One study indicated that a majority of first-year students (59%) gained weight, and that the average gain was almost five pounds. Of course, this raises a number of potential issues. Body image concerns and eating disorders are serious matters and apprehension about appearance or potential weight gain can heighten the pressures some students may feel to adhere to an unhealthy weight standard.

While weight gain is not as much of an issue as the idea of the "freshman 15" might indicate, weight, body image, and general appearance are major issues for many students; fears of not "fitting in" or of being perceived as unattractive may significantly impact the choices they make. Therefore, an institution's focus on stewardship of the body, healthy habits, and emotional health is tremendously important in helping first-year students navigate an emotionally challenging time. If appropriate attention is given to helping them develop knowledge and behaviors supporting healthy eating, exercise, and a healthy self-concept, it will enable students to live healthier and more meaningful lives.

What Can Parents Do?

If there is one redeeming quality in the movie *Revenge of the Nerds*—and indeed, it is a stretch to call anything associated with this film redeeming—it is that the movie points to the critical stage of a college experience when students first come to campus. Research has shown that initial college experiences often have a significant impact across a spectrum of social, personal, and educational outcomes.[12] These experiences include what is traditionally thought of as orientation, occurring prior to the beginning of the school year and extending through the first year of college. Finding an institution that fulfills your child's needs by practicing hospitality during orientation is one of the most critical aspects of the entire process. *Revenge of the Nerds* is filled with countless absurdities, but even within this mix of myth, adolescent fantasy, and outrageously stereotypical misrepresentations of college life lies a glimpse into a basic human need: the need to belong. As Christians we recognize this need as part of our created interdependence on God and his people in Christian community. We are created for community, not for isolation or individualistic lives. Reuben Welch's classic phrase "We really do need each other"[13] provides a useful slogan for campus community. A simple but profound summation of this notion is found in the Psalms: "How good and pleasant is it when brothers live in unity" (133:1).

What role should parents play in supporting their children as they make the initial foray onto a Christian college campus? There are several things you can do to help your child navigate the transition from high school to college.

The big day has arrived and you have just survived carrying boxes, a TV, a couch or your old recliner, several suitcases, and a small but heavy refrigerator up three flights of stairs on what has to have been the hottest August day in years. Your son is at college, you've moved him in, helped him set up his room, and he is off to begin the school's orientation program while you exhaustedly ask yourselves, "So what do we do now?" Your role as parents may be changing, but it is far from over.

I am often asked what the biggest changes in the college experience have been over the span of my career. In my opinion, the three biggest changes are: the role of technology in the delivery of education and in the everyday lives of those involved in education; the role parents play in their children's college experience; and the amount of stuff students bring to college.

How many parents can relate to the differences between the year when I first went to college in 1981 and today? In 1981, email didn't exist, there were no cell phones, no phones in our rooms (in fact, we had just three landlines that serviced a residence hall of 270 men), and no personal computers. Instead of bringing me to campus, my parents gave me a credit card (which I was to send back to them) and told me to call once I arrived. Everything I took to campus fit into my two-seater car and consisted of two suitcases, a sleeping bag, a stereo, and a hot air popcorn maker that made me a very popular guy on my floor. This August, students will arrive on campus with their entire families in SUVs or full-size vans, some of them pulling utility trailers, crammed with belongings containing the very latest in technology, not the least of which will be multiple means of staying connected with their parents. And, to top it off, all of this has to fit into a room that hasn't changed in size from when I started college.

What about the changing role of parents in the day-to-day lives of students? Parents are taking a much more active role in their children's college education then they have in the past. For the most part, this is not a bad thing, as long as the focus is on nurturing and supporting them so that they can thrive in college. The key is to nurture and show support but to maintain enough distance for them to develop healthy personal, spiritual, and intellectual independence. Many parents do this very well, but there is a growing trend for parents to stay overly involved in their children's college experience, thus impeding rather than encouraging their development.

As I have mentioned previously, parents of traditional-age college students have been described in recent years as "helicopter parents"[14] in that there is a growing tendency to hover over their children and stay overly involved with their collegiate experiences. Let me give you an example of one such parent. Recently, I was taking questions after a presentation I made to parents at a summer orientation session when I was approached by a mother and her daughter. After introducing herself and her daughter to me, this mom posed this dilemma: "We have met our roommate and it isn't going to work out." As I began to try to understand the concern, I directed my comments to the daughter but the mother did all of the talking. Instead of helping her daughter navigate this situation, the mother was trying to eliminate a potential threat to her daughter's happiness at college. On the surface this may seem like a normal parenting task, but in reality it interfered with a valuable opportunity for the daughter to learn how to deal with difficult situations. This daughter needed to learn through the process of addressing her differences with the roommate and developing strategies for dealing with interpersonal problems. Parents must recognize the need for their children to lead in these kinds of situations and to offer support but not to solve their problems for them.

Roommate conflicts are not the only situations where helicopter parents have a tendency to intervene inappropriately. Another common example is when a student has a problem with a faculty member. It is not uncommon for students, especially at the beginning of their college experience, to question faculty. Students may perceive unfairness related to grading practices, number and difficulty of assignments, and the amount of work required. In the vast majority of cases, this angst results from college being harder and more demanding than high school and students' varying degrees of preparedness for this new level of academic challenge. Most often what the student perceives as unfairness is simply a demanding subject and a professor who is challenging them to excel academically. In most instances, these issues can be resolved with a one-on-one meeting with the faculty member. This is certainly true in a Christian college setting where the faculty members are to be committed to combining their academic training with their faith commitment.

So, if your daughter or son calls to complain about a course or professor, your first response should be to ask if she or he has met with the faculty member outside of the classroom. It is natural to want to intervene and contact the professor yourself, but doing so will block a valuable learning opportunity provided by these informal conversations with committed faculty. Worst of all, if you choose to intervene for them, you will send a strong message that you do not believe they are capable of handling their own problems.

This is a good place to discuss the Family Educational Rights and Privacy Act, more commonly referred to as FERPA.[15] This act became law in 1974 and its basic purpose is to protect the privacy of college students. FERPA deals primarily with educational records and who has the right to have access to them. The right to decide access transfers to the student at age eighteen. In a nutshell, FERPA limits what colleges and universities are allowed to share with parents without permission from the student. Students may sign a FERPA waiver (available at most registrar offices) granting parents the right to receive protected information. This would be a good topic to discuss with your daughter or son before she or he arrives on campus. Without a waiver, school officials, including faculty, are limited in how much information they can share from students' educational records.

FERPA can at times create tension between parents and the institution their child is attending, as it may seem as if the institution is not willing to be a good partner with parents. This does not mean that you should not communicate with the college, but you do need to know that Christian colleges are bound by FERPA in the same way that public institutions are and that it may limit what information you receive.

It is also essential to realize that the amount of involvement by parents is just as important as the type of involvement. With today's technology, it is easy to stay in constant communication with your daughter or son at college. I know of cases where parents talk with their children on cell phones multiple times a day. This access makes it easy for the student to rely too heavily on parents. Furthermore, if they are overly connected to friends and family at home, they will not connect as readily with people in their new location. Balance is the key. You want to stay involved to the point where you know what's going on in your daughter's life, but not to the point where she is relying too heavily on you and is not able to take full advantage of the educational opportunities.

Another important consideration is how often your child should come home for a visit. The first semester is a critically important time for developing friendships and a sense of belonging. Coming home too soon or too often works against these important developments. As I have said, homesickness is a real issue with many new college students, but maintaining too tight a connection with parents and home often worsens the situation. Here again, the key is balance. You don't want to sever the connection with your son but rather to modify it, showing your involvement and support but allowing him freedom to establish himself in his new setting.

Conclusion

The beginning of your daughter or son's time at a Christian college is critical. These college communities welcome their newest members through orientation programs designed to embody Christian hospitality. As parents, your desire should be to support your children as they embark on this new chapter of discovery and growth. There will be changes in your relationship, but these changes are part of the natural maturation process and can be an important part of faith development. Trust in the truth found in Scripture that reads, "Train a child in the way he should go and when he is old he will not depart from it" (Proverbs 22:6). You have given your children a good, solid foundation for the Christian college experience. Now it is time for them to take on more ownership for this next phase of their spiritual journey.

Prosperity Abounds

Rethinking Success during the College Years

I f Washington, D.C. is considered the epicenter of American
political life and New York City the epicenter of American
financial life, perhaps Boston, Massachusetts, and Cambridge,
Massachusetts in particular, are considered the epicenter of
American academic life. As the home of Harvard University,
Cambridge has served as the educational home for almost four
hundred years to future leaders ranging from Nobel Laureates
to heads of state. Supported by the largest endowment in
American higher education, Harvard has come to embody
what many Americans think of as academic success. However,
despite its enviable position, academic success, even at Harvard,
proves difficult to define.

This question of success forms the heart of Alek
Keshishian's film, *With Honors*. The film follows the lives of
four Harvard seniors as they come to terms with the meaning
of success through an unexpected teacher—a homeless man
who initially took up residence in the boiler room of Harvard's
Widener Library. The film begins with one of these students,
Everett Calloway (played by Patrick Dempsey), announcing
on his campus radio show that seniors had only 180 days to

complete their thesis projects before the so-called "powers that be" decide if they "are destined for greatness or mediocrity." He then goes on to announce that in order to be among those destined for greatness, students need to be willing to "crush" anyone who gets in their way.

Among the students subscribing to the harsh yet real view of life espoused by Calloway is his roommate Monte Kessler (played by Brendan Fraser). A political science student and aspiring diplomat, Monte's thesis is well on its way to being complete when the hard drive on his computer crashes. Fearful that the one hard copy in his possession leaves him vulnerable to other unforeseen challenges, Monte heads out into a driving snowstorm to make more copies. While bantering during this trek with his third roommate, Courtney Blumenthal (played by Moira Kelly), Monte drops his thesis only to have it fall through a vent into Widener Library's boiler room.

While Courtney distracts the guard at the front desk, Monte searches for the lone copy of his thesis and finds that it has fallen into the hands of a homeless man, Simon B. Wilder (played by Joe Pesci). Instead of willingly returning the thesis, Simon strikes a deal with Monte, the return of "one page for one thing."

Although the two men initially see one another as means to ends (Monte gives Simon various things ranging from a glazed doughnut to new underpants and in return Simon gives back the pages), the film eventually portrays how they come to view their developing relationship as the end. The turning point comes when they realize that, while Monte resents his father for abandoning him and his mother when he was young, Simon himself abandoned his wife and son. Human relationships by their very nature demand vulnerability—a lesson not lost on Monte or on the fourth roommate, a fledgling premed student named Jeff Hawkes (played by Josh Hamilton).

As the movie progresses, it also becomes apparent that Simon's health is deteriorating. Having breathed in asbestos in the shipyards of Baltimore, it was just a matter of time until Simon succumbed to mesothelioma. On the night before his thesis is due (a thesis which he started anew after meeting Simon), Monte is faced with a difficult decision—either he could take Simon to see his estranged son in Maine or complete his thesis on time, thus qualifying him to graduate with honors. Monte, along with his three roommates, chooses to take Simon to see his son.

Although Monte does not graduate with honors from Harvard, the movie infers that he graduates with honors from life. Academic success comes to be defined more by the contribution he was able to make to others than his ability to simply get ahead of them. While a laudable challenge to the academic culture in which we find ourselves, perhaps *With Honors* could go one step further. The movie could challenge viewers to think about not only how we define academic success but also the reason we pursue it. While seeing our relationships as being more important than our individual efforts is commendable, in the end it does not prove to be enough. In particular, Christian colleges and universities by their very nature are obligated to tell their students why their best efforts are important and valuable.

The Significance of the Christian College
Certainly not all students subscribe to the notion that part of academic success is the willingness to crush anyone who might

get in their way, but most are susceptible to the viewpoint that more is better. When I say "more," I mean higher grade point averages, more activities, and larger forms of involvement. Schools are encouraging students at younger ages than ever before to develop portfolios demonstrating what makes them unique or exceptional. The ideal student graduating from high school today may look something like a straight-A student, captain of an athletic team, first chair in the student orchestra, student body president, and someone who is highly involved in a local charity. While these efforts prove to be rightful uses of time and effort, they should not be the only considerations when judging student success. In order to cut through the admittedly impressive façade of such résumés, one must ask how students are still significant if their portfolios fall short of this standard of excellence.

The definition of success varies from student to student and from college to college. It must vary because of the manner in which each one of our children were created. Genesis tells us that God created humanity in his own image. By virtue of our fallen and finite nature, no one person represents God's image in its totality. No one person can represent all of God's character. For example, some students are given abilities with musical notes. Others are given abilities with numbers. Still others are given abilities with words. Of course, some people possess these gifts in greater measure than others. However, when students stand together, they are able to recognize the diversity of gifts that God has given them. The challenge for a particular Christian college or university is to recognize these talents and encourage students to cultivate them to the best of their abilities.

Another way to look at the giftedness of our students is in relationship to their calling or their vocation. If God created each one of them with certain gifts, God also has a certain plan for how those gifts are to be used. Some students arrive at college with clear plans for how to use their giftedness, but experience has also taught me that Christian colleges and universities should be prepared to provide their students with a host of opportunities to explore these gifts. These opportunities will certainly be woven into chapel services and academic courses; but many will come through co-curricular programs such as service-learning and study abroad. These kinds of programs allow students to become active participants in particular communities and thus help them discover how their giftedness can be used to serve others.

At this point, however, I come up against the same challenge that faces a movie such as *With Honors*. Is it enough for students to see success as using their gifts and talents to serve others? Or is there some greater purpose of our giftedness? For the Christian college or university, the answer is yes. Remember—our highest calling as human beings is to offer praise and worship to God, and serving the needs of others becomes one of the most important ways we express that calling. Christian colleges and universities seek to cultivate awareness within students of their gifts and talents and how those gifts and talents can be used to serve others. But service to others is not the end of our efforts. Rather, we serve others because such efforts bring glory and honor to the God who created us all.

Keeping in mind the command to glorify God, a Christian college or university should be intentional about challenging its students. Being stretched is often an uncomfortable process. However, we should not see academic formation as any different than the training athletes undergo. Like athletic coaches, teachers should be constantly challenging their students to both recognize and exercise their giftedness, which may require reasonable levels of discomfort. Being gifted in a particular area does not mean that the expression of those gifts comes with ease. Parents need to be supportive of this type of challenge. Indeed, I would even argue that parents should be somewhat concerned if their children are not reporting on a consistent basis that what they are going through in college is raising significant questions about their abilities. Up to a point, the Christian college experience should be characterized by the discomfort caused by the challenge to work harder than students have had to in the past.

A professor who is not challenging students to stretch their abilities is not only doing them a disservice but is proving dishonorable to God. The created giftedness of a student is a valuable trust, as illustrated in the parable of the talents. Christ tells of a master getting ready to go on a trip. He gives one servant five talents, one servant two talents, and one servant one talent, noting that the number of talents given to each servant was proportional to his ability. When the master returned, the first two servants offered their master twice the number of talents he had originally given them—products of their wise investment efforts. However, the third servant had buried his one talent in the ground and thus had only one talent to offer in return. Christ tells us that the master responded, "You wicked, lazy servant! So you knew that I harvest where I have not sown and gather where I have not scattered seed? Well then, you should have put my money on deposit with the bankers, so that when I returned I would have received it back with interest" (Matthew 25:14-30). For our purposes, the enduring lesson here is that teachers are entrusted with the enormous responsibility of cultivating the giftedness of their students. Failure to do so is irresponsible to the gifts God has given the teachers themselves.

However, parents should also expect that the professors' level of challenge is comparable to their level of support. Because the created giftedness of students is a valuable trust, teachers are called to know their students well enough to know when encouraging words are more appropriate than challenging ones. Here, again, professors and coaches must employ similar training strategies. If coaches push their athletes too little, skills never develop. However, if coaches push too hard, their athletes may become discouraged or even sustain injuries that prove detrimental to previous gains. This dynamic has been proven very effective in the classroom as well. I encourage parents to expect that their daughters and sons will not only be challenged but also given the support necessary to learn and grow through these challenges.

The message of success offered by the Christian college or university is thus one where each student is challenged and supported to cultivate his or her talents so that those talents can be used in service to others and, ultimately, in praise and worship of God. Movies such as *With Honors* offer a helpful corrective but do not go far enough. Students are not here to learn simply to serve other members of the human race; rather, their service to the human race is a gift they offer first and foremost to God.

What Does the Literature Say?

Although there is no doubt that a college degree affords important material, employment, and social benefits, the designs for Christian educators extend far beyond these temporal concerns. Institutions themselves are prone to define success by their most easily measured characteristics, for instance, graduation rates. While this is, of course, an important measure of institutional effectiveness, it is a poor proxy for knowing if students are truly learning. This is especially true if students are growing in their understanding and acceptance of what it means to be a disciple, to follow and serve Christ in the home, the workplace, and the world beyond. Given the costs and the importance of higher education, it is understandable that many develop a narrow definition of success in college. Rather than being concerned about positive, whole-person development, students and their parents are tempted to focus on "bottom-line" issues and activities that enhance a résumé or increase potential employability and earning power. These are important concerns and certainly valuable byproducts of higher education, but they are unsuitable as a primary target, especially for Christian higher education.

A key purpose of Christian higher education must be to prepare students to serve the world and the Kingdom for the glory of God. In order for this to occur, students must be challenged and have experiences that let them apply and test what they learn in the classroom. These experiences provide a laboratory where your daughter or son can experience the kind of deep learning which characterizes thoughtful, reflective, and resilient Christ-followers.

The deep-learning process is set in motion when a student begins to feel discomfort or, in developmental terms, "disequilibrium." This most often occurs when a person recognizes that she or he has insufficient abilities, knowledge, or understanding to successfully negotiate an experience. This discomfort acts as a motivation to adjust or adapt to meet the challenges being faced, whether they are intellectual, spiritual, or emotional. The process of adaptation ultimately leads to what we label growth or maturation. If this idea seems strange, consider how it plays out in our faith development. It is when we begin to understand that our lives are incomplete and that our resources are not sufficient to meet our needs that we begin to really know our need for Christ and his redeeming work in our lives. We must experience this disequilibrium, this sense of incompleteness, before we are able to respond to the gospel in a manner that brings about change in our lives. This is but one example of the developmental process. For college students, this process is taking place in virtually all realms of their lives: intellectual, social, moral, physical, and spiritual.

Consider what first-year students go through as they are flooded with awkward situations, challenges, and new experiences. Whether these challenges produce or stunt growth is determined in large part by students' perception of their ability to meet them and the confidence they have in the support that is available. One of the important goals of college educators as they work with students is finding the ideal balance of challenge and support.[1] On the one hand, the unchallenged student will simply not learn or grow, as it takes healthy challenge to force her or him to "reach," which in turn leads to the adaptation or learning discussed above. On the other hand, if students are so overwhelmed by challenge that they outrun their resources (or perceived resources), they may shut down.

Rather than experiencing growth, they may actually regress to safer places and positions. This is often what happens to the students who drop out of college during their first semester—they simply feel ill-equipped to face what they see ahead of them, so they quit.

How parents prepare their children for these challenges has a great impact on how successfully students will respond. This is one of the chief concerns with "helicopter parenting." This hovering style of parenting can hurt students by taking away their opportunities to be stretched and thus adapt to new challenges; it also communicates to students that they are not capable of solving their own problems without assistance. Christian colleges generally do an admirable job of creating an environment where students are both exposed to challenges which will stretch them and provide the support necessary to nurture growth. There is probably no stronger warning I would give than this one: allow your child to work through the challenges and difficulties inherent in the college experience on her or his own. If your goal is to cultivate a young person capable of functioning confidently and effectively in the classroom, workplace, church, and home, you must avoid the temptation of moving in to help them resolve their problems. You can pray for them, encourage them, share your experiences with them, and certainly love them, but you must first let them take responsibility for their own experiences.

Consider some of the college experiences that can contribute to students' uneasiness or distress. For instance, they may have their beliefs challenged in the classroom or by living with someone from another denomination, another culture, or even someone who does not embrace faith in Christ. While these things may be disconcerting, they are also the very things that cause students to think deeply about what they believe and why they believe it. Students often find that the simple paradigms with which they have been able to navigate life's challenges successfully in the past are now inadequate for the new ideas and experiences to which they are being exposed.

The goal here is not to tear apart a student's orthodox beliefs and then leave them alone to rebuild their broken intellectual or faith world. No, in fact this is one of the chief benefits that Christian colleges offer. These institutions have been formed to challenge students in a manner that helps them to clarify, solidify, deepen, and own their beliefs in a way that would not be possible without honest evaluation and reasonable testing. Rather than insulate students from the dangers of the world, Christian colleges are attempting to strengthen and equip them through programs, experiences, and other resources so when they graduate they are prepared to deal with such obstacles successfully. A Christian understanding of success does not portray the believer as "hunkered down," resisting the onslaught of the world. Rather, Scripture reminds us that a vital and serious relationship with God is one that will allow us to "overcome" and to be "more than conquerors." I would argue that no entity better balances challenge and support than the Christian college. The mission of Christian higher education is to produce graduates who will not just survive or be successful in their own right but who will live lives that bring glory to God. Its focus on learning combined with faith, and the attention it gives to worship and fellowship as part of the formal learning process, creates a rich and healthy academic environment.

Christian colleges commonly use additional programmatic opportunities and initiatives to expose students to a variety of important areas and to accomplish important learning goals. These programs are often grouped under the heading "experiential education." By this, I am referring to experiences in which a student participates in some sort of planned activity for which she or he has prepared in advance and which is followed with a processing time or reflective experience.

Study Abroad

Due to the strong positive impact of study abroad experiences on students, participating in a semester overseas increases the likelihood that students will have a successful college experience.[2] According to research conducted at Florida State University by James Posey, "The most often cited gains or benefits related to study abroad participation are in the areas of maturity, language proficiency, increased knowledge of a specific culture, and global-mindedness."[3] Posey continues by postulating that "study abroad could theoretically lead to increased psychological and skill growth, thereby leading to positive educational and employment outcomes."

Additional studies confirm the benefits of study abroad on a successful college experience. In an extensive study, Mary Dwyer and Courtney Peters found that "study abroad positively and unequivocally influences the career path, world-view, and self-confidence of students."[4] Students overwhelmingly agreed that studying abroad dramatically influenced their personal development. Over 95% of students who studied abroad agreed that the experience increased self-confidence, increased maturity, and made a lasting impact on their worldview.[5]

Parents would be wise to encourage their daughters and sons to make participation in such opportunities a priority. This is especially important considering that when students graduate, it will be into a world that is increasingly interconnected and globally oriented. Perhaps more importantly, these experiences can do much to fuel our efforts to follow Christ's command to "go into all the world."

Mission Trips

While mission trips may have some of the same features and benefits of study abroad programs, they should be considered on their own merits. The number of people participating in short-term mission trips has exploded over the last decade.[6] This phenomenon reflects the importance that Christian colleges place on providing short-term mission trip opportunities for their students. Clearly, participation in short-term missions has the potential to impact students significantly. One study on the impact of short-term missions on a group of young people discovered that the experience enhanced the participants' spiritual lifestyles.[7] In this study, 47% of the students said their time spent in prayer increased somewhat, and 6% noted a significant increase. Further, volunteerism increased somewhat for 33%, and increased significantly for 19%. Additionally, this study showed gains in other important areas such as church involvement, interest in poor countries, and advocacy for the poor. In discussing the impact of short-term missions on college students, David Johnstone, Associate Dean of Students at George Fox University, explains that "particularly for college students, short-term cross-cultural experiences have the potential for being one of the most formative and 'worldview shaping' pedagogical experiences of their college career."[8]

The short-term mission trip provides a unique learning experience offered by many Christian colleges that is not available at secular institutions, except occasionally as offered by campus ministry groups. While these experiences are also valid and valuable, they do not have the benefit of institutional support or of being embedded in a campus culture that values these experiences and works to incorporate them into the lives of its students.

Service-Learning

Like short-term mission trips and study abroad, participation in service-learning can provide a wonderful enhancement to a student's experience. Service-learning, or the idea of formally linking an academic class with a service component, has been repeatedly recognized as a powerful teaching tool. The idea that service-learning seeks to "equally benefit the provider and the recipient of the service as well as to ensure equal focus on both the service being provided and the learning that is occurring"[9] demonstrates why it is a practice that fits so well with the values of Christian higher education. Through service-learning experiences, students will accomplish multiple aspects of a successful Christian education including serving the local community, testing course content by means of practical application, and becoming more aware of the needs around them. Service-learning experiences are a wonderful means for helping students learn how to connect belief and behavior, a primary goal for Christian educators.

Students who participate in service-learning opportunities are impacted in a number of positive ways, including increased grade point average, critical thinking skills, self-efficacy, leadership, and plans to participate in service after college.[10] Not only are such experiences powerful learning opportunities, they also provide a powerful witness of Christ's love to the people and communities being served.

Selecting a Major

In a chapter devoted to understanding college success, I would be remiss if I ignored the important issue of choosing a major field of study. The choice of a major has an enormous impact on what a student will learn and experience in college. Identifying an academic pursuit provides students with a necessary academic goal and infuses purpose and excitement into the college experience. Beyond this immediate benefit, evidence suggests that major selection strongly relates to what students experience after college. Ernest Pascarella and Patrick Terenzini explain that undergraduate field of study has substantial impact on a student's ability to find employment, their future occupational status, and eventual earnings.[11] While I have already made the point that success as defined by Christian colleges is more holistic than job placement and earnings, securing solid employment that fit a student's gifts, skills, and sense of calling is important.

Successful major selection has also proven to increase a student's likelihood of remaining in college. In other words, students who declare majors early are more likely to remain in school because of a heightened sense of purpose and vision. Studies indicate first-year students who had declared a major were more likely to come back for their second year.[12]

Obviously, in order for students' college experience to be successful, they must finish their degree. From the perspective of a Christian college, successful holistic development of students is hindered when students do not select majors that are well suited to them. A student's ability to decide upon a major that fits with her or his gifts, skills, and desires is critical in ensuring long-term life and career satisfaction.

What Can Parents Do?

Parents can play a major supportive role in assisting their daughter or son to navigate the sometimes uncertain waters of career or vocational choice. This choice is one of the most critical elements of the collegiate experience. A healthy exploration of the myriad of options can help your child take full advantage of her or his years in college and successfully prepare for life after graduation.

There are three major categories of students: first, those who decide on a major before coming to college and stick with this choice; second, those who decide on a major prior to college but change their major one or more times after coming to school; and finally, those who come to campus without having decided on a major. All three need guidance in pursuing their vocational calling, even those who have a predetermined major and follow this academic plan through graduation. They still need assistance in testing their decision and in moving through the job or graduate school search process. Likewise, those who change majors or those who have difficulty in deciding on a major need similar advice and counsel as they weigh their options and make decisions. Parents can and should play an important supportive role in these processes.

I have three specific recommendations for parents regarding your child's selection of a major. The first is to commit this process to prayer. Pray for your daughter's guidance, pray for your discernment in providing assistance, and pray that her collegiate experiences will begin to show her God's intended path for her life. The second is to encourage her to access the appropriate support services available to her on campus. Christian colleges are very interested in the vocational preparation of students and have a vested interest in this process for their students. Finally, encourage her to be an explorer and to take full advantage of the opportunities that come with attending a liberal arts Christian college. Advise her to engage across a spectrum of classes and activities that will help her explore options, test and discover strengths, and prepare her for any number of vocations.

A good place to start in this process is to recognize the spiritual dimension involved. As Christian parents, we often recognize the increased sense of importance and urgency associated with this process for our children, but we also have an increased sense of assurance that God is intimately interested and involved. We know from Scripture that God has plans for our individual lives (Jeremiah 29:11), that God as our benevolent heavenly Father wants to give us good gifts (Luke 11:11-13), and that ultimately if we place our trust in God, all things work for good (Romans 8:28). In other words, God has a plan and is willing to give us what we need to cooperate with God in accomplishing that plan. If we place our trust in God, we are assured that all things will work out for good. These are incredible promises from a trustworthy God who is "looking for ways to show himself mighty on our behalf" (2 Chronicles 16: 9). Therefore, the most important support you can give your daughter in her vocational search is prayer. Ask God to guide her as she seeks God's will, and ask God to equip you as you support her in this process.

Now let's turn our attention to some specific ways you can support your child once she or he has gone to college. There are two very important sources she or he needs to tap into that are available on every college campus: the career development office and the academic advisor. Both of these resources will be invaluable in helping your child explore academic majors and career options based on these majors. Both of them are available to all students regardless of when they decide on a major and should be utilized by all students throughout their college career.

If your daughter has decided on a major before she comes to campus, one of the first persons she should interact with is her academic advisor. This person will work with her to develop and implement a four-year academic plan that will help her graduate on time, take full advantage of her academic abilities, and introduce her to the available resources. Advisors can also play an important role in identifying internships as well as in the eventual job search. The career office can assist those with declared majors by helping them develop a four-year vocational plan that includes career exploration during the early stages of college. It can also help students obtain career-related internships and assist college seniors with services related to the job search such as résumé development, job search strategies and tactics, and interview preparation.

If your son is on the other end of the spectrum and does not have a clear sense of his academic direction, he should start immediately with the career office. One-on-one career counseling can be a great place to help him gain a sense of who he is and point him toward majors that fit his interests and passions.

He will also be given helpful tools to assist in this process. These tools can range from personality assessments such as the Myers Briggs Type Indicator[13] to specific personal strengths analyses such as Strengths Finder.[14] Additional assessments such as Career Direct[15] and the Campbell Interest and Skill Inventory[16] can provide information about potential career tracks that match personal interests and strengths. These tools, administered by the career office, can help your son identify his God-given passions, explore career options based on these passions, choose an academic major, and eventually commit to a vocation. This process of career exploration will allow him to become engaged with an academic advisor who will help him solidify his choice and guide him through to graduation.

If your daughter has a preselected major but then chooses a different track after a semester or two, then both her academic advisor and a career counselor can assist in this process as well. Any change in major has to include an academic advisor. If this is the route your daughter pursues, she should start with her current advisor who can direct her to other potential majors within the discipline and to think through the implications of the decision. That person will also likely suggest that your daughter visit the career office to get their assistance in choosing a new major. Changing majors is not uncommon and when done thoughtfully and for the appropriate reasons can be a healthy realigning of a student's vocational path. I survived this process as an undergraduate and actually changed majors twice during my first year with no inclination as to my future career in higher education.

Parents of non-declared majors as well as those whose children change their majors, especially those that change later in their college careers, are often concerned about the potential side effects. The difficult thing is that there really is not a hard and fast rule as to when a student needs to choose a major or how often or when she or he should change her or his major. In most circumstances, I would suggest that the sooner these are done the better. Each student's experience will be unique, and I can tell you success stories of students who did not choose a major until their junior year, students who changed majors multiple times, and some who even changed during their junior or senior year. However, as a general rule, the sooner your child selects and sticks with a major, the more likely she or he will be to graduate in four years. The key is to know your child and the circumstances surrounding why she or he has not selected a major and then intervening if appropriate. Generally, I would be more concerned with a student who cannot decide on a major at the end of the second year than I would be with a first-year student.

Another vital component in the search for a vocation is exploration. One of the hallmarks of the liberal arts tradition is that students are exposed to a wide breadth of knowledge through a variety of academic disciplines as well as a depth within their concentrated studies. This breadth and depth approach provides students with opportunities to explore many fields that can have a direct impact on them vocationally regardless of (or in conjunction with) their major course of study. Sometimes students overlook their general education classes or get impatient to get into their major classes and, as a result, do not fully engage the liberal arts curriculum. General education courses are an integral component of a well-rounded education that produces well-rounded persons. This is particularly true in the Christian college setting, where the inextricable relationship shared by faith and learning provides the ideal context for nurturing whole persons capable of developing real-world solutions to real-world problems.[17]

Involvement in the co-curricular program at his Christian college can also have a significant impact on your son's vocational pursuit. I am not suggesting he get involved in every opportunity that becomes available, but that he choose a variety of programs to help expand his experience and his worldview. Encourage him to consider his options wisely and then to choose those programs that match his passions, interests, and abilities. In a healthy balance, these co-curricular experiences are invaluable in augmenting classroom learning and providing opportunities for him to explore new experiences. The types of experiences that I am advocating include such things as small group Bible studies, on- and off-campus ministry groups, intramural sports programs, special interest clubs, international and domestic short-term mission trips, leadership roles, and study/travel abroad opportunities. The key is to encourage him to pick and choose so that his involvement is at a healthy level and augments his academic experience rather than supersedes it.

The process of encouraging your child's vocational pursuits is an important part of your role as parents. It is a process that needs to be bathed in prayer. Additionally, you need to become informed so you can encourage your child to connect with the appropriate campus services and staff. Finally, show your encouragement and support as your daughter reflects upon what these experiences teach her about herself, the world, and God's purpose for her.

Conclusion

While serving the communities in which we live is good and noble, Christian colleges and universities offer that such a commitment is not enough. Service to others is not the end in and of itself but rather an important means of offering praise and worship of God. *With Honors* makes a good point. Too many members of our society think that success is predicated on our ability somehow to defeat those individuals who would stand in our way. But God asks more of us. Even good practices such as service to others can be made into an idol if fueled by mere human desires and motivations. Christian colleges and universities are called to help cultivate within their students greater desires and deeper motivations. Our ability to offer praise and worship to God through various means such as service then becomes the true measure of success.

A TIME TO CRY

Crisis and the College Experience

In 1995, John Singleton's movie *Higher Learning* struck a prophetic chord. By the end of that decade, students, teachers, and administrators would come to feel the grip of a seemingly never-ending wave of school violence. In the fall of 1999, Columbine High School in Littleton, Colorado would serve as the backdrop for a horrific scene where two students killed eleven of their fellow classmates and one teacher. In the fall of 2006, an adult gunman burst into a one-room Amish school in West Nickel Mines, Pennsylvania, took the female students hostage, and then killed five of them before he committed suicide. In the spring of 2007, a student at Virginia Tech University in Blacksburg, Virginia killed thirty-two of his classmates and teachers before committing suicide. Unfortunately, this list of events does not do justice to the many other students, teachers, and administrators who have also been caught in the grip of violence. This list simply captures the blunt force generated by a few of the largest events. Still today, my thoughts and prayers are with the families impacted by all of these tragedies.

I would like to promise that such events will never happen on Christian college and university campuses, but such a promise would prove meaningless. I have spent countless hours thinking about ways to make campuses safer, knowing that this aspiration, while perhaps more important than any other I hold, is also illusive. Each year, college and university communities unknowingly welcome people who may pose a threat to themselves as well as those around them. A former colleague, a clinical counselor, once said that it was not the individuals that he knew that caused him to lose sleep at night but the individuals he did not know.

John Singleton's hauntingly prophetic film brings this reality of the individuals we do not know to the forefront as it is a film about a community that does not know itself. In the absence of any larger community, its students live in isolated sub-communities defined by race, gender, and extracurricular interests. Isolation breeds fear, which over time breeds violence.

Set at the fictional Columbus University (a school probably not accidentally named for Christopher Columbus and looking remarkably similar to the University of Southern California), *Higher Learning* follows the lives of three students as they seek to find their home away from home. While Singleton's film does prophetically foreshadow what was to come, it also uses shamelessly stereotypical characters to tell its story.

First, Malik Williams (played by Omar Epps) is a talented track star who comes to Columbus on an athletic scholarship. He quickly begins to feel as if being an athlete for a major university is simply a high-profile version of indentured service. He may have received a scholarship, but his ability to stay in his coach's graces is entirely determined by his performance on the track. As a student, Malik feels he is never taken seriously. He is simply written off as an athlete whose presence needs to be tolerated off the track so that the university can reap certain benefits from his athletic performance. With little initial guidance from the university, Malik falls prey to the influence of Fudge (played by Ice Cube) who convinces him that his racial identity as an African American is the reason behind both the favor and the oppression he receives at Columbus.

Second, Kristen Connor (played by Kristy Swanson) is a white female from Orange County, California. Although her family recently faced some financial hardships, Kristen apparently lived a relatively charmed life. She is eager to get involved at Columbus but quickly realizes that the social life is defined by far more tragic opportunities than what she experienced in high school. Her friends prove to be rather vain groupies of a vulgar social fraternity. One night, Kristen drinks too much and then finds herself the victim of sexual assault by one of these fraternity members (in tragic reality, an all-too-common occurrence). In order to find solace, Kristen then falls prey to Taryn (played by Jennifer Connolly) who convinces her that the reason behind the oppression she has faced is the gender dynamic in place at Columbus. Taryn then goes so far as to try to become sexually involved with Kristen.

Finally, we meet Remy (played by Michael Rappaport), a young man who initially wants simply to focus on his studies. A consistent series of run-ins with Fudge and his friends prompts Remy to seek community among a group of white supremacists. Remy then falls prey to their influence as they convince him that the oppression he faces is the result of reverse discrimination. This rhetoric fuels Remy's anger to the point that he eventually shoots several members of the Columbus community. The movie eventually leads us to a scene where we see

Kristen and Malik, two students who initially come to college full of high aspirations but who are now deeply entrenched in their sub-communities, meet at a makeshift memorial established on behalf of their slain classmates.

Perhaps the only voice offered by the university is that of Professor Maurice Phipps (played by Laurence Fishburne). Otherwise, students are generally left on their own to find their way at a university whose sense of community appears to go no deeper than the geographical boundaries defining the campus. If people really are created for community, this film aptly illustrates how they may fall prey to any number of sub-communities, some constructive and some destructive.

What Is Christian Community?

If Christian colleges and universities prove to be nothing else, they should be worthy reflections of the kind of community we first encounter in the church. The church is where we first learn that we are called as a people to offer praise and worship to God. The church is where we are initiated into the body of Christ through our baptism. The church is where our faith is nourished by the practice of the Lord's Supper and the hearing of the biblical story of creation, fall, and redemption. People who are members of various Christian college and university communities are not immune to the possibility of a crisis. The difference is how our identity as members of the body of Christ helps us prepare for, endure, recover from, and even grow through a crisis.

First, Christian college and university communities are defined by an acute awareness of humanity's God-given potential. These institutions exist on behalf of the church to help humanity more fully realize what it means to be created in God's image. In Genesis, we read: "Then God said, 'Let us make man in our image, in our likeness, and let them rule over the fish of the sea and the birds of the air, over the livestock, over all the earth, and over all the creatures that move along the ground.' So God created man in his own image, in the image of God he created him; male and female he created them" (Genesis 1:26-27).

People often have a hard time appreciating what it means to be created in the image of God. Either practical atheism impairs our ability to realize that something greater than us exists or some form of low self-esteem propels us to think of ourselves as being much less than our created potential. We were each unique creatures and called to offer our lives in praise and worship to God. However, this calling is not one that is simply given to us as individuals. In his book *Engaging God's World*, Cornelius Plantinga Jr., president of Calvin Theological Seminary, claims that "we image God when we live in loving communion with each other. Because God is triune, the image of God is social as well as personal."[1] Just as the body of Christ is social as well as personal, so the Christian college is social as well as personal. Part of how the Christian college prepares its members for a crisis is by first practicing hospitality in such a way that the diverse reflection of God's image in all members of the community is appreciated. The way we welcome one another then directly relates to how we respond to one another in times of crisis.

Second, Christian college communities are defined in part by an awareness of the fallen and depraved nature of humanity. Too often, sentimentality or being nice for the sake of being nice permeates Christian environments from the church on down. Too often, our fear of conflict propels us to gloss over the harsh realities of a fallen world. Shortly after we realize that humanity was created in God's image, we must realize that humanity has also fallen from grace. Genesis 3:23-24 tells us that, as a result of the fall, Adam and Eve, as well as all of their successors, were banished from the Garden of Eden. Neither the church nor the Christian college can afford to ignore this reality. To ignore it is to disregard the depth of the sacrifice Christ made on our behalf. Dietrich Bonhoeffer, the famous German theologian, referred to this as "cheap grace"—more wishful thinking on our part than the true transformation of grace. Because of this understanding, Christian colleges seek to embody through their policies and practices a deep awareness of human depravity, if for no other reason than that such an awareness is necessary to anticipate the redemption which God alone offers us.

Finally, Christian college and university communities are defined by an appreciation for the transformative power of the redemption offered by Christ's sacrifice. In the Gospel of John we learn that: "For God so loved the world that he gave his one and only Son, that whoever believes in him shall not perish but have eternal life. For God did not send his Son into the world to condemn the world, but to save the world through him. Whoever believes in him is not condemned, but whoever does not believe stands condemned already because he has not believed in the name of God's one and only Son" (John 3:16-18). God's intention is not to condemn his creation but to redeem it. While God cannot overlook our depravity, he does not want our depravity to tell the last chapter of our story. Ultimately, we are called back into full communion with God and with one another. In the same work quoted earlier, Plantinga writes that "in the fellowship of the Christian community, the redeemed person embarks on a life's adventure—to discover the purposes of God and make them her own; to discover the ways of the kingdom and follow in those ways; to uncover the 'mind of Christ' and to strive to become likeminded."[2] Knowing this, Christian colleges and universities need to possess policies and practices that help them see that the end result of any crisis is ultimately redemption.

John Singleton is right to characterize today's university as being susceptible to a crisis, and no school is immune to the possibility. But the Christian college, by virtue of its very nature, should embody a story that not only appreciates its members' God-given potential but is also keenly aware of the depths of human depravity. However painful, a crisis should not catch us off-guard. Neither should a crisis have the final say. In the end, God calls all of us to come to terms with the power of Christ's crucifixion and the transformative power that comes from God alone. As a result, the Christian college should not be a lonely place where students struggle to find community among a varied array of sub-communities. Rather, the Christian college seeks to be a community defined by its calling to deepen within each of its members an appreciation for how we can all work together to offer praise and worship to God.

What Does the Literature Say?
When considering what college to attend, students and their parents often make assumptions about the institutions of

interest and about the experiences that they will have at these schools. College-bound high school students are unlikely to be very concerned about the safety of the campuses to which they are drawn. Typically, they are much more interested in things like potential roommates, the availability of desired majors and classes, residence life amenities, and the types of activities in which they will participate. They are much more likely to dwell on their social and academic fitness than on issues of physical or emotional well-being. While safety concerns may rank somewhat higher for parents, their modest unease is generally satisfied by simple reassurances from campus tour guides or admissions materials. Although the integrity of these individuals and materials is not in question, it is quite likely that those speaking or writing on behalf of these institutions are not entirely aware of the real threats and potential dangers.

The unfortunate but unavoidable reality is that college campuses are not problem-free or crime-free, and students must exercise caution even though day-to-day campus life appears innocuous. I am not by any means implying that students should walk around their campuses in fear or suspicion of those around them. However, I am advising that healthy caution and a realistic understanding of potential threats and problems is prudent.

Several factors can contribute to safety concerns. First, the very atmosphere that is so attractive to most of us is simultaneously a threat. Because of the trusting community atmosphere that is often one of their most delightful features, Christian college campuses can be an easy target for people who would take advantage of the inclusive nature of college students. This manifests itself in a variety of ways, ranging from manipulative but marginally legal sales schemes intended to separate students from their money to much more serious criminal activity which threatens students' physical and psychological well-being. Sometimes those threats come from individuals beyond the immediate community, though the threats may even come from individuals inside the community.

The second factor that can negatively impact campus safety is the developmental level of college students. Put simply, all students are not at the same level of maturity. While some are almost fully developed adults in their cognitive and emotional abilities, many are not. An important purpose of college is to help students in the maturation process. However, while this process is taking place, young adults are more prone to engage in unhealthy risk-taking. Additionally, students are more susceptible to a host of other problems. Alcohol and substance abuse are two especially pernicious problems that can endanger both the student and the individuals with whom she or he associates.

Finally, we know that some of the most important developmental processes taking place are those involving growth in emotion management and the development of healthy relationships. Often, these are among the most exciting aspects of college life. But unusual problems or shortcomings in these areas can make some students more likely to misinterpret emotional cues or behave inappropriately. Most typically, these sorts of behaviors are evidenced in misunderstandings, arguments, hurt feelings, or frustration, but on very rare occasions they may escalate into dangerous situations. Thus, it is important to know that the institution your daughter or son attends takes these matters seriously and has the appropriate staff and programs to address them in a proactive and effective manner.

A parent can find out about such readiness in several ways. First, an informal evaluation of the importance placed on student development and campus safety will be an excellent indication of how well a college is prepared to deal with conflict. It is also helpful to know that there are federal and state statutes that require institutions to report crime statistics to the government and, consequently, the public. The Cleary Disclosure of Campus Security Policy and Campus Crime Statistics Act, more popularly known as just the Cleary Act, requires an annual report. Every college in the nation that accepts federal student aid must publish annual statistics detailing crimes on their campuses. These statistics provide a starting place, but it is important to note that there are significant questions regarding their accuracy and their helpfulness. Surprisingly, studies have shown that very few people ever actually look at this information.[3]

To give you a sense of the national picture, in 2008 the government reported that there were 1,255 arrests for college-related illegal weapons possessions. Illegal drug possession or use yielded 24,047 more arrests, and the government reported 49,353 liquor law violations.[4] While these figures may be alarming, one must consider them in context: in 2007 there were over eighteen million students in America's colleges and universities. Furthermore, approximately 6,600 institutions report this information each year. It is safe to assume that the values embraced by most Christian colleges, as well as the type of student who tends to be attracted to these colleges, makes the likelihood of encountering such problems much lower.

However, the student or parent who assumes that attending a Christian college will immunize them from crime or danger is making a significant mistake. The reality of contemporary American life makes it unwise to assume complete safety in any situation. Any college setting represents a collection of young adults whose age makes them more prone to risk-taking behaviors and who are in the midst of one of the most intense periods of emotional and interpersonal development.

I have considered some very serious issues; but perhaps the most common potential dangers of the college years are emotional rather than physical. College students are discovering their identity, learning to manage and master their emotions, and developing mature relationships.[5] Progress in these realms is often hard-won under the best of circumstances. The typical student will move through the maturation process by sorting out beliefs, relationships, and self-understanding. For some, though, such struggles will be dramatic and will involve problems with potentially life-altering, even life-threatening ramifications.

Among the more common issues that students deal with are stress and relationship problems. Concerns about student mental health have been reported in both the popular and academic press. *U. S. News and World Report* indicated that approximately ten percent of college students have considered suicide, forty-five percent experience depression at a level making it difficult to meet the demands of college, and over thirty percent find themselves feeling frequently overwhelmed.[6]

Likewise, the annual Freshmen Survey conducted by HERI in 2009 reports a number of similar findings. The results, representing over 27,000 first-time, full-time, first-year students from seventy-eight institutions in the category "other religious colleges," provide the following picture. Over twenty-seven percent of these students report that their parents, though both alive, are divorced or living apart. Almost thirty percent indicate that they frequently or occasionally drank beer during the past year and thirty-six percent say that they frequently or occasionally drank wine or liquor during the same period. When considering these figures, keep in mind that for the vast majority of those responding, the year in question was their senior year of high school, when they were well underage for legal alcohol consumption. In fact, ninety-eight percent of the respondents indicate that they are age nineteen or younger, which offers even more grounds for pause.[7]

The problem of alcohol abuse and underage drinking on college campuses is well documented and was discussed in chapter three. The link between substance abuse and mental health is equally well established. College students who misuse alcohol are clearly more vulnerable to a host of other mental, emotional, and safety concerns. There is no doubt that one's coping skills are impacted negatively, which may help explain why over twenty-nine percent of the students in the HERI study "frequently felt overwhelmed by all they had to do," and seven and a half percent reported feeling depressed. Finally, when one is struggling with emotional concerns or simply engaging in practices detrimental to mental health, it also impacts one's outlook and perception of the world. Considering that one of the great hopes of Christian higher education is to equip students to serve as "salt and light" in a hurting world, it is particularly disheartening to hear that twenty-seven percent of the first-year students enrolled in America's religious colleges and universities believe that, "realistically, an individual can do little to bring about changes in our society."[8]

One of the biggest mental health issues for students in college is depression. In *College of the Overwhelmed*,[9] Richard Kadison, the previously mentioned director of mental health services at Harvard University, contends that student mental health concerns are increasing in colleges across the country. He offers that "despite this appearance of comfortable status, secure environment, and a pleasant social world, a multitude of hidden problems have caused a steady and alarming rise in the severity of students' mental health problems."[10] In a recent study, one of my former graduate students, David Downey, discovered through his research that it may be very hard to recognize students who are struggling with depression just by their levels of campus involvement.[11] He found that a significant number of students reporting depression still maintained a fairly high level of campus involvement. Thus, it is critical that faculty and staff at Christian colleges and universities are equipped to recognize and refer students who are exhibiting symptoms of depression.

Unchecked and untreated, depression often leads to lower academic achievement, dropping out of college, and in severe cases, even suicide.[12] Most Christian colleges take these issues very seriously and provide training for student and professional staff who have significant contact with students. Additionally, almost all of these colleges and universities have counseling centers, and many offer access to medical personnel who have been professionally trained to assist with such concerns.

However sad it may be to think of a college student dealing with depression during these best years of their lives, it should be encouraging to know that students who are helped with such problems during these formative years will be much better equipped to function successfully after college. It is critical to remember that we are part of a story defined not only by the creation and the fall, but also the power of God's redemption. No Christian college or university is immune to these kinds of challenges. The difference is between a community that assumes a crisis will never strike and a community that is hopeful yet prepared for any challenge it may face.

What Can Parents Do?

When I first started my career in student development as a residence hall director over twenty years ago, I had a recurring fear of experiencing a residence hall fire. I used to imagine how I would react to a fire, and I took fire safety measures, such as practicing how to use a fire extinguisher and making sure the residents engaged in regular fire drills, very seriously. I took pride in knowing the students could exit the residence hall in well under the five-minute target given to us by the local fire marshal.

Today, I am still vigilant about fire safety but now have several additional concerns. This increased anxiety has been fueled by horrific media images from incidents such as those mentioned earlier in this chapter. It has also been fueled by the overall increase I see in events that happen on campuses across the country about which the general public never hears. As I interact with colleagues from other colleges and universities and compare notes, I note a growing sense of urgency that threats to student safety need to be taken seriously by all parties.

You may be taking a big sigh of relief, thinking that surely this somewhat bleak picture does not apply to the nurturing environments found on the average Christian college or university campus. Even though Christian institutions may experience less crime, assuming that they have developed immunity to these issues is another example of "bubble effect" thinking and can lead to a false sense of security for both students and parents.

This is true regardless of the location of the college. Historically many Christian colleges and universities, like their traditional liberal arts counterparts, were located in rural settings where students could be insulated from the distractions and trappings of larger cities. This isolation, while for the most part supportive of the educational process, can also create a misguided sense that students do not have to think about their personal safety. Each campus will have its own unique safety concerns. Additionally, today's students are incredibly mobile, and with this increased mobility comes greater exposure to the gamut of potentially dangerous situations. Likewise, urban campuses have their own specific safety challenges. They have to maintain tighter security measures to limit unauthorized access to campus as well as more tightly monitor the comings and goings of their students.

Three persons or groups need to take students' personal safety very seriously. The first is campus personnel. The second is you as parents. The third and most important are the students themselves. Most likely, the first group is very convinced of this already. I am not aware of any Christian college or university, or for that matter any college campus, which does not have strong staff, programs, policies, and other resources in place to help keep students safe. Likewise, parents for the most part are very concerned about their children's safety—this is one of the areas in which I receive the bulk of parental phone calls. The ones I am most worried about are the students.

I am consistently amazed at how many students seem indifferent to their own safety as well as that of their fellow students. I observe or hear about students who run on secluded roads by themselves at night (with iPods in their ears), prop open the locked exterior doors to their residence halls, fail to lock their residence hall rooms or vehicles parked on campus, and other risky behaviors. As I have talked with students and analyzed these tendencies, I have identified a couple of common elements that contribute to students' casual approaches to safety. The first is the myth of the indestructibility of youth. Students, like most young adults, have the mistaken notion that they are indestructible and nothing will happen to them, or if it does, that they will be okay. The second element is that they are genuinely unaware of the potential ramifications of their behaviors. I am always surprised, when I talk to students about dangerous behaviors, how often they are sincerely surprised that what they are doing could be considered dangerous. I was recently on campus about 9:45 P.M. when I noticed a single female student jogging alone. Knowing this student fairly well, I pulled ahead of her and waited until she came to a well-lit corner and talked to her about violating what I considered to be a "Safety 101" issue. She was really surprised that I would think she was unsafe jogging alone in the dark. I then followed her to the residence hall and prayed that she understood. But I am not sure she did.

Let me address one of the most difficult subjects that needs attention—sexual assault. As I mentioned earlier, the impact of the fall is probably most evident in relation to the havoc it has caused with sexuality. The world in which we live has turned an experience designed to be the physical consummation of marriage into an act offering little more than personal gratification. As a result, people often come to view others (and even themselves) as mere objects, with the most grotesque expression of this objectification being sexual assault. College and university campuses are certainly not immune. In fact, approximately one in four college women will be the victim of sexual assault during her college career.[13] Despite our common perceptions that the perpetrators of these crimes are generally strangers, approximately eighty percent of these assaults are committed by acquaintances. Given the epidemic nature of this problem, I believe that Bonnie S. Fisher, Francis T. Cullen, and Michael G. Turner's report for the United States Department of Justice entitled *The Sexual Victimization of College Women* should be required reading for anyone who cares about the well-being of college students (both women and men). This report is free and available for download at http://www.ncjrs.gov/pdffiles1/nij/182369.pdf.

While even our best efforts may not eliminate this kind of activity (although we will keep trying), students can make choices that will reduce their chances of getting hurt. Please take the time to talk with your daughter about this reality. (Please note that although male students are statistically less likely to suffer from this kind of criminal activity, such instances can occur.) Help her develop a sense of discernment concerning who she spends time with and where she spends it. Help her understand that alcohol greatly diminishes her level of discernment and her ability to protect herself. Explain to her that if she says "no" to a sexual advance, she has every right to expect that such an utterance will be honored. If she is a victim, work to cultivate the kind of relationship that will allow her to come and talk with you. At the same time, keep in contact with college officials in offices such as campus safety or campus police, the health center, and student development so that they can be part of the process of healing and justice.

As parents, I am not sure what we can do to help our children get past the indestructibility of youth myth except to challenge this thinking (the previously mentioned statistics concerning sexual assault should help), to support them through the maturation process, and to be in consistent prayer for their wisdom and well-being. Perhaps the only sure cure for youth is age. However, I do think parents can help their children realize that they are ultimately the ones most responsible for matters of personal safety. The safest campus in the world cannot protect students from themselves if they make unwise choices. The key is to stay engaged with your daughters and sons and keep having these conversations about personal safety. This sounds simple, but as the parent of a college student, I know how easy it can be for her to tune me out when, in her words, I begin "sounding too much like a dad." I actually take this as a compliment and take as many opportunities as I can to remind her to be safe. Even though she gives me a hard time about it, I think my daughter actually appreciates my concern, and my prayer is that she is taking my fatherly advice to heart. You need to find the balance between teaching your daughter or son to think practically about safety without stifling their natural development and enjoyment of campus life.

As parents, be as informed as possible about the pertinent safety issues at your child's campus. Start with the obvious ones, such as urban versus rural campuses and on-campus or off-campus living accommodations. Then do some in-depth homework and access public information about the campus. Information related to the Cleary Act is easily accessible and most campuses have it available on their Web sites and/or through their public safety or campus police departments. This information is being made even more accessible with the 2008 reauthorization of the Higher Education Act which requires colleges and universities to create a consumer information Web site that is easily accessed and provides specific information, including many safety-related issues.[14]

Remember, this online information can provide some insight into the safety concerns on a campus, but it may not provide a complete picture. I also suggest that you address any concerns or questions directly to staff members at the college. Residence life staff members such as hall directors are a good place to start, but there are others including campus police/safety staff, admissions staff, and other student development personnel such as the director of residence life and the dean of students. These campus representatives will be able to provide you with answers to your questions. When it comes to the safety of your daughter or son, the only bad question is the one that does not get asked.

Parents should also become familiar with the counseling and health centers. Many Christian colleges and universities have worked tirelessly over the last several years to make certain that the number of mental health counselors is keeping pace with the increased demand from students. These staff members are often not only highly trained in various counseling practices but also in how those practices are woven into the fabric of the Christian faith. For example, a Christian counselor working with a student struggling with an eating disorder would not only understand the biological and psychological dimensions of such a challenge but also the spiritual dimensions and ramifications of this issue. The ultimate goal would not be just to help the student to overcome the eating disorder but also to learn how his or her life fits into God's larger plan for redemption.

Given the reality presented in this chapter, keeping pace with this surging demand is no small challenge. As I noted, some students are bringing significant emotional challenges with them to college and others experience these challenges during their college years. Some mental health professionals indicate that this generation of students is far more comfortable seeking out these kinds of services than previous generations. The social stigma once identified with seeing a counselor is fortunately subsiding. As a result, the demand on most campuses is increasing dramatically. By being familiar with the mental health services available on your daughter or son's campus, you will be better equipped to encourage your child to seek these services as needed.

Much of the same can be said for the health center. Staff members serving in a health center often include registered nurses, nurse practitioners, and physicians. They stay up to date on information concerning the health challenges of college students. While they are readily available to help treat the ailments students are facing, they often prefer to serve as campus health educators. Instead of simply treating ailments and illnesses after they arise, many health center staff members find it more productive to teach students how to take charge of their own well-being, perhaps even eliminating problems before they start. This wellness approach to health has tremendous benefits that can be very beneficial to students both during and following college. It is important that the health center receive up-to-date health information on each student, including preexisting conditions and medicines. This vital information, allowing campus health services to provide ongoing care, is guarded closely by HIPAA[15] regulations and will be kept strictly confidential. Again, you can play a critical role in encouraging your children to be informed about the health services available to them. Becoming familiar with the health services will allow you to direct your son to the appropriate care when you receive the 2:00 a.m. call informing you he has been throwing up and doesn't know what to do.

We all hope and pray that our students will never be the victims of violent crime, but in a fallen world, even under the most ideal circumstances, such things are possible. We must rely on God while at the same time being diligent to make wise choices that protect us from dangerous situations. I liken this to the advice Jesus gave his disciples: "I am sending you out like sheep among wolves. Therefore be as shrewd as snakes and as innocent as doves" (Matthew 10:16). Encourage your child to engage fully in the Christian college experience, but also to be aware of potential dangers.

Conclusion

One of the most significant measures of the character of a Christian college or university is how that community responds to a crisis. This responsiveness depends entirely upon the fabric of the community and the Christian narrative that shapes it.

Does the story we inhabit merely acknowledge the realities of God's creation and humanity's fall or does it also have a place for God's active hand of redemption? Columbus University, as portrayed in John Singleton's *Higher Education*, is a congregating point for a host of sub-communities. In contrast, this narrative—the biblical narrative of creation, fall, and redemption—is what brings members of Christian college and university communities together in the hope that tomorrow can, in fact, be greater than today.

The Cultivated Vocation

Expectations of Life after Graduation

The 1980s witnessed the rise of a group of young actors and actresses that eventually came to be known as "The Brat Pack." Members of this group such as Judd Nelson, Ally Sheedy, and Emilio Estevez would go on to play a number of roles over the course of their still active careers. But they are best known for their roles in two early films, *The Breakfast Club* and *St. Elmo's Fire*. *The Breakfast Club* tells the story of a diverse group of high school students who find themselves thrown together for various reasons in Saturday detention. Richard Vernon (played by Paul Gleason), the school administrator assigned to supervise them on that Saturday morning, tells them to write an essay on how they view themselves and their worth as people. The students reject this request and simply argue that regardless of what they think of themselves, society is still inclined to define them by superficially manufactured labels such as jock, geek, princess, and misfit—labels teenagers are still too often willing to embrace.

In many ways, *St. Elmo's Fire* replays these same themes of identity with a collection of recent college graduates. In contrast to their high school counterparts, the college students are not quite as susceptible to the labels. Instead, they are more inclined to define themselves by their aspirations for independence and careers. Success in both of these arenas is often defined by the ability to accumulate wealth. *St. Elmo's Fire* thus tells the story of seven friends as they struggle to find their way during their first year after graduation from Georgetown University. Still living in the Georgetown neighborhood in Washington, DC, these friends each represent an archetype of the routes young people take following graduation. In the end, the film leaves me with more questions than answers. As each of the friends comes to realize that the route they have taken is flawed, they admit that life after college is simply hard and that perhaps the best days of life are now behind them.

For example, the two most successful members of the group are Alec Newberry and Leslie Hunter (played by Judd Nelson and Allie Sheedy). Living together in a fashionable loft apartment, Alec works in the office of a Democratic representative. The impeccably dressed and equally well-spoken Leslie proves to be the ideal girlfriend and possible wife, but only in concept. In the end, Alec trades his political convictions for a higher salary by moonlighting on the weekends for a Republican senator. In addition, his superficial commitment to Leslie is betrayed by his sexual encounters with other women. Eventually, the façade of perfection comes crashing down, leaving the two of them confused and questioning their future.

A more humorous reflection of this theme is presented by the character Kirby Kegar (played by Emilio Estevez). Kirby holds a number of positions in the film, all designed to win the affection of a young physician he originally met as a college student. Kirby cannot seem to decide whether he should pursue a career as an attorney or as a physician. In the end, he has no real commitment to one profession or the other. The only goal he has in mind is selecting a career that will make him worthy of this young woman's affection. When he realizes that her affection is driven by more than professional status, Kirby becomes disoriented and also left with more questions than answers about the future of his life.

Finally, the character in this film who appears to undergo the greatest angst is Kevin Dolenz (played by Andrew McCarthy). An aspiring writer, Kevin is depressed by the fact that the newspaper he works for has assigned him to write obituaries. Instead of writing about the recently deceased, he aspires to write about the meaning of life. This pursuit escapes him for most of the movie until his piece concerning this grand question is finally printed. He thinks this level of success will finally win the heart of the previously mentioned Leslie Hunter, the woman he has secretly loved for several years. In the end, he finds that all she is willing to offer him is a one-night stand that has more to do with her frustration with Alec than any love for him. This realization also leads him to the conclusion that life after college and perhaps even the meaning of life is hidden in a confusing array of harsh details.

The Significance of the Christian College

Perhaps the creators of *St. Elmo's Fire* are correct. At times it does seem as if life is defined by a host of harsh details. The previous chapter bore witness to the reality that trials and tragedies are often woven into even the Christian college experience. Illness, unemployment, and unfulfilled aspirations for love are just some of the challenges we may face over the course of our lifetimes. But this movie's most disconcerting quality is the lack of purpose or calling that permeates it. Pain and suffering are unbearable if we lack a greater calling for our lives. As Christians, our calling is first and foremost to offer praise and worship to God. We fulfill this calling in different ways, but learn to see all of our efforts as part of that larger plan.

As I have discussed, common worship experiences found in venues such as chapel should then define both what goes on inside as well as outside the classroom. The lessons that teach students to offer their lives in praise and service to God should be present from the opening moments of orientation and extend seamlessly across the campus. Simply to offer such opportunities in the senior year is not sufficient; they need to be woven into the fabric of the student's experience from the very beginning.

Assuming your daughter or son has experienced a well-ordered Christian education, the senior year should then afford her or him with some unique opportunities. One of the goals of Christian colleges is to help students know how to integrate themselves into enriching and sustaining communities beyond graduation. In the following sections, I will talk about these opportunities and communities in greater detail.

First, the Christian college should serve as a means of helping students see that their calling and thus their identity is inextricably tied to the relationships that they share with other members of the body of Christ. In Galatians 3:26-29, the Apostle Paul admonishes: "You are all sons of God through faith in Christ Jesus, for all of you who were baptized into Christ have clothed yourselves with Christ. There is neither Jew nor Greek, slave nor free, male nor female, for you are all one in Christ Jesus. If you belong to Christ, then you are Abraham's seed, and heirs according to the promise." On our own, each one of us represents what it means to be created in God's image. However, when bound together by our baptism as members of Christ's body, we come closer to approximating the overwhelming grandeur of God's own identity. In and through the church we gain a fuller understanding of our true identity. The world presents harsh challenges. But our presence in the body of Christ gives our lives purpose and meaning in good times and bad.

Second, the Christian college also needs to provide its students with opportunities to think through the array of other relationships they may pursue after graduation. For example, your daughters and sons will probably get married (however hard it may be to believe). Many will become parents (however harder that may be to believe). Others may see singleness as part of their calling in life. They will become members of particular professions. Although these relationships are important ways we can offer praise and worship to God, they can also become idols. Dating relationships, marital relationships, children, and work can all usurp our relationship with God if they are not understood in the proper context. The Christian college should teach its students to view these admittedly significant roles as secondary extensions of their identity as members of the body of Christ. Keeping our relationships in proper order is not only critical to helping us be faithful Christians, but also to be faithful spouses, parents, friends, and employees.

Finally, the Christian college should offer students the opportunity to think through what their relationship to the college will look like following graduation. Graduates of a particular institution have historically referred to it as their *alma mater* or "nourishing mother." What does it mean for a Christian college to be referred to in this manner? Too often, recent graduates think of themselves as newly-minted targets for college development officers assigned the responsibility of raising money. While sacrificial giving is one way that graduates can strive to guarantee that the opportunities provided them will be there for the next generation, it is only one small part of the identity of a recent graduate. The Christian college wants its students to understand that many of them will be called to serve on various boards and as mentors or even interviewers for future generations of prospective students. Some may one day return to campus as professors and/or administrators. Graduates are not simply individuals who once took up residence on campus, but valued stakeholders in charting the future of their *alma mater*.

Unlike the purposelessness portrayed in *St. Elmo's Fire*, the Christian college has the responsibility to instill in its students an identity rooted in the fellowship of the church. If our students and your children fail to properly understand that relationship, the chances of them being able to faithfully navigate the myriad of other relationships in their lives are reduced. While the Christian college is entrusted with the responsibility of fostering the next generation of citizens, spouses, parents, and employees, its success is first and foremost defined by the way it points its graduates toward the lives they are to lead as members of Christ's body.

What Does the Literature Say?

For a number of years, developmental psychologists have had a difficult time definitively establishing the end of adolescence.

It is fairly simple to determine the starting point—it begins with the fanfare and fireworks of puberty. But determining when someone "stops being an adolescent" and "starts being an adult" is a much more complicated proposition! In recent years there has been a shift away from viewing this transformation as a distinct ending of one stage and beginning of another. Now, we are much more likely to envision a gap between adolescence and adulthood. And, this gap, running roughly from ages 19 to 29, is bridged by a transition increasingly being referred to as "emerging adulthood." This label points to a gradual shift that takes place over time and results in a person who is fully ready to acknowledge and accept traditional adult responsibilities.

As recently as thirty to forty years ago, there was a common expectation that when a person finished high school, she or he would go to work, into the military, or off to college. If a person went the college route, it was expected that immediately after college she or he would find a job, settle down, and either get married or set up housekeeping for themselves. Well, times have changed.

Consider marriage, the most certain marker of adulthood in previous decades. In the past, most people married in their early twenties, began a career and family, and basically settled into the lifestyle of their parents. But in recent decades, the age at which people marry has risen considerably. In 1970, the average age for marriage for women in the United States was twenty-one; it is currently twenty-six. Between 1970 and 2002, the average age at which people bought their first homes rose from twenty-nine to thirty-three. One of the most visible changes is the length of time that emerging adults live with their parents. About twenty percent of twenty-six-year-olds still live with their parents.[1] A 2004 survey of college students revealed that approximately sixty percent planned to return to their parent's home after graduation.[2]

Whether or not they live with their parents, individuals in this age range (just like college students) have far more contact with parents than was typical in the past. Part of this is surely a result of the ease and economy of contact afforded by mobile phones, email, text messaging and other forms of electronic communication. However, it also appears that there is a change in the nature of the relationship between parents and their children. While many of us enjoy this ongoing connection and the ability to stay in touch with older children, it is important that our role does not shift from one of support and sounding board to one of entanglement. By these patterns of constant interaction and by continuing to live at home, college students may be in danger of delaying the establishment of healthy independence.[3] Of course, our ultimate task as parents is to help our children develop a healthy and responsible identity so they can function successfully as adults. Thus, as hard as it may be, we must carefully guard against practices that will diminish the likelihood of this happening.

In his recent book *Souls in Transition: The Religious & Spiritual Lives of Emerging Adults*, Christian Smith defined emerging adulthood as a period of "intense identity exploration, instability, a focus on the self, feeling in limbo or in transition or in between, and a sense of possibilities, opportunities, and unparalleled hope . . . often accompanied . . . by large doses of transience, confusion, anxiety, self-obsession, melodrama, conflict, disappointment, and sometimes emotional devastation."[4] While this picture may or may not accurately describe your child, it does describe many of their peers as well as the culture that surrounds them. And, to the point of this chapter, it impacts the way they experience the transition from college to life beyond the campus.

A student's senior year at a Christian college can provide wonderful preparation for this important life transition. College seniors are concerned about many practical issues such as: What will I do for a job? Where will I live? How will I make friends? Where will I find a church? Some of these seemingly simple and mundane questions can be quite intimidating to those who have never had to deal with them before. It is wise for colleges to provide transition programming designed to help students with these questions and fears.[5] Many colleges that have long understood the need to have orientation programs for first-year students have just recently begun to recognize that the transition out of college is every bit as exciting, frightening, mysterious, and challenging as the transition into school. As a result, most colleges have developed programming—sometimes part of the formal curriculum, sometimes part of the co-curriculum—to equip graduates for this transition. As parents, encourage your daughters and sons to avail themselves of these opportunities.

In addition to these practical concerns that are often so strongly felt by students, other important issues need attention. This is an important time for students to contemplate what they have learned and experienced during college and what it will mean for their lives in the future. This is a difficult process because it requires significant energy and attention at the same time students are completing degree requirements, looking for jobs, applying to graduate schools, and trying to soak in the last remnants of their college experience. John Gardner, perhaps the nation's leading authority on college transitions, wrote: "Indeed, the consensus that has developed among scholars and practitioners in higher education is that the most basic need of seniors is for opportunities for reflection on the meaning of the college experience, integration and closure, and holistic support during the transition to post-college life."[6]

This transition represents a key opportunity for both colleges and parents. For colleges, the responsibility is to provide structured experiences assuring that this reflection occurs and that it is well guided.

For parents, this represents a golden opportunity to further solidify an adult-to-adult, "eye-to-eye" relationship with your children. One of the key developmental tasks of college students is to "develop mature interpersonal relationships."[7] Perhaps no relationship in this transition is more important or more complicated than that of a college student with parents. Be intentional in treating your child like an adult and communicating your desire to talk about her or his experiences. By doing this, you can aid your child's ability to make sense of what she or he has learned and experienced during college, and also deepen your relationship. This can be an incredibly rich and rewarding experience as the relationship moves from "caretaker to child" to "peer to peer." While it will be many years before they have the experience and knowledge that you do, your acceptance of them as responsible, mature (although novice) adults is critical and will go a long way toward stimulating their independence. Parents who navigate this transition successfully serve their children well and position themselves optimally to be an important influence on and resource to their adult children.

Most seniors and recent grads will put a great amount of effort into finding a job. However, the goals for students seeking jobs vary. For some this will be an effort to find a long-term position in the career realm. For others, the goal may be a job in which they can gain experience that will further prepare them for the kind of work they want to do in the future. Still others may see this first job as simply a placeholder, a way to pay the bills while figuring out what they really want to do with the rest of their lives. Ironically, research indicates that while students generally feel prepared to enter the workplace, underclassmen often feel better prepared than upperclassmen.[8] This discrepancy likely results from the fact that, for the senior, the reality of getting a job and having their readiness tested in the workplace is looming just over the horizon. It may also be a result of increased maturity and a more accurate understanding of the challenges associated with the world of work.

It is very easy for students making this transition to base career decisions simply on economic concerns: either taking a job because it will provide the kind of lifestyle they desire or because it will at least pay the bills. This is why it is imperative for colleges, especially Christian colleges, to help their students (starting with underclassmen) discern their calling. This means assisting students in determining what they need in order for their lives and their careers to be meaningful and beneficial to God's Kingdom. This is a challenging and complex task. As theologian William Spohn puts it: "Faced with a multitude of career options and often uncertain about their own gifts and aspirations, graduates can frequently let other voices determine what they will do. Family expectations, the opinion of peers and the demands of the marketplace often dictate what shape their lives should take."[9]

Given current economic realities, students do, of course, need income to allow them to live responsibly and independently and to contribute to the church and the needs of others. The magnitude of this need is brought into even sharper focus when we consider that in 2008 the average debt for a student leaving college was $23,200.[10] Clearly, preparing students for a successful transition to the workplace and grounding them in a biblical understanding of vocation is critical for both parents and Christian colleges.

While many students go straight from college to work, others choose to continue their education. About twenty-two percent of college graduates go on to graduate or professional degree programs.[11] Because they have completed a college degree, the academic world is a familiar one. Despite this familiarity, however, they will still have to make a number of adjustments.

First, the nature of graduate education is generally quite a bit different than undergraduate education. There is a much higher level of expectation that students will contribute to their own learning. Courses often are conducted as seminars, which means that a great deal of course time may be spent discussing readings or application of concepts and less time spent with a faculty member simply covering course material. Additionally, the workload, and particularly the reading load, can be much more intense. Students may be required to read a great deal in very short periods of time. Many graduate programs also place much greater emphasis on papers than on tests; therefore, good writing skills are particularly important. Finally, graduate students are expected to assume more responsibility for managing requirements, deadlines, and other academic matters. Unlike most undergraduate faculty, it is unlikely that graduate faculty will give frequent reminders of due dates, student responsibilities, or other course matters. Students are simply expected to know the syllabus and meet the requirements.

Although there are many fine Protestant and Catholic graduate programs, graduate education in the United States is largely offered by public universities or private secular universities. Thus, there may be a number of related adjustments for students who have attended Christian colleges as undergraduates. Because it would be impossible here to address the variety of lifestyle challenges that a student may face, suffice it to say they will not experience the widespread similarity of beliefs and values they experienced as undergraduates. Thus, graduate students need to be very intentional in seeking fellowship and support. Many church-sponsored organizations provide such opportunities for students. And, while the myriad of challenges in a secular institution may be more obvious, the graduate experience affords an outstanding opportunity for committed Christians to live out and test their beliefs. The one basic recommendation I would offer to Christian students entering such programs is really the same one I would offer students in Christian institutions: make your faith, church involvement, and connection to other believers a key priority.

Finally, graduate school can be a wonderful time of learning and growing in faith, knowledge, wisdom, and intellectual ability. In order to assure this, I would encourage students to enter carefully but also with excitement and anticipation. This is a strategic opportunity for Christians to unite with non-Christians in a common, meaningful pursuit. Furthermore, as students challenge and support one another and grow together in friendship, it is a magnificent opportunity for Christians to be the body of Christ, a tangible symbol of his love.

What Can Parents Do?

This discussion reminds me of a recent conversation I had with my college-age daughter. She was experiencing some angst during a conflict involving relationships with several friends. The issues were fairly complex, and she was trying to analyze her feelings and roles as well as trying to interpret the actions and motives of the others involved. As she was telling me the details, I was inwardly beaming, realizing that she trusted me enough to share these issues with me and, thus, I became a little distracted. I was taken off-guard when she asked me the fatal question, "Dad, what do you think?" I had a deer in the headlights moment and blurted out this gem of wisdom, "Honey, being a grownup is hard." Thankfully I was able to recover quickly and offer what I hoped were meaningful insights into her situation.

As I reflect on this now, I realize that my ill-conceived wisdom regarding the difficulty of being a grownup was actually not that far off, although perhaps too simple in the context of the conversation with my daughter. The issues facing the characters in *St. Elmo's Fire*—Who am I? What will I do with my life? With whom will I spend my life? What is my purpose in life?—are identical to the issues our children will face as they navigate through college and life after graduation. For parents, this is a process that requires the willingness to transition from parenting an adolescent to coming alongside an emerging adult. This may sound easy, but as I have witnessed others go through this process and as I am living through it with my own daughter, it is much more difficult than it first appears. But it is not impossible. If we understand that the end product is seeing our children become the people they were intended to be, it is definitely worth doing and doing well.

It must be said that the process of the parent-child relationship morphing into that of peers should only go so far. The relationship will change, but I do not believe it is healthy for parents and children to become totally equal peers. Each child will develop at a unique pace; therefore, the rate and level of this transformation will also be unique. The delays associated with emerging adulthood may very well mean that your daughter or son will achieve a sense of autonomy at an older age than you did. Following are several suggestions for you to consider while you and your child negotiate the transition through emerging adulthood.

First, realize that this is a necessary change. It has to happen for your daughter or son to become the functioning adult God has intended. The author of Proverbs admonishes us to "train a child in the way he should go, and when he is old he will not turn from it" (Proverbs 22:6). We are to be very intentional in instructing our children in how they should live, so that when they are older, they can base their lives on biblical truth. It can be very difficult to allow this person whom we have nurtured and guided for eighteen to twenty-two years to experience pain, stress, and potential failure. After all, who cares more for them than we do? During their transition into adulthood, however, it is our responsibility to let them face their important life decisions as Christian adults.

Second, be actively engaged in transforming your role throughout all of the college years. The issues of vocation, marriage, study abroad, and others do not just emerge in the senior year and should be addressed throughout college. As parents, we need to encourage our children to engage with these decisions as underclassmen so they will not feel pressured to make all of their big choices in their final days of college.

Third, be prepared for them to follow their own vocational dreams rather than the ones you have for them. Inherent in the process of letting your children take ownership in decision-making is the possibility that they may not choose the life path that you would have expected or desired. Some will make what may seem to be a radical vocational choice during this process. The essential issue is *how* they live out their vocational calling rather than the specific choices they pursue. Ask yourself, are they pursing God's call for their lives and using the gifts and talents God bestowed upon them?

Ephesians 4:11-12 reminds us that the body of Christ has many roles and within this diversity the key challenge for both Christian parents and Christian educators is to prepare "God's people for works of service." Ask yourself if you turned out the way your parents thought you would. I know I did not. My childhood and early adulthood on the family farm was not a likely preparatory setting for my career in Christian higher education. If my mom or dad thought I would someday make a likely candidate to serve as a college administrator and faculty member, they never mentioned it to me. The key for my parents then and for you as parents of college students now is to help prepare your children for whatever God has in store for them. The emphasis should be on how they live their lives and whom they serve rather than on your vocational dreams for them.

Once you have realized that this transition through emerging adulthood is a good and natural process, you can do some practical things to nurture the change. I would suggest you begin by taking every opportunity to help your daughter or son reflect on her or his calling. As discussed earlier, Christian Smith reminds us that this transitional period is one filled with both positive and negative elements. The sense of hope and possibility combined with confusion and anxiety[12] dictate the need for your daughter or son to reflect consistently on this process of transition. This will allow her or him to connect the dots and provide a useful context to make sense out of all she or he is going through at this point in time. Without reflection, these experiences can seem disconnected, confusing, and unfortunately to some, unnecessary.

Reflection is particularly important for this current generation of college students, as they are not necessarily practiced in this art. This generation is the most technologically saturated to date, making them very event focused. They tend to have just enough attention to focus on the moment, and then the next experience is on them and they are swept away. It is vitally important to help them slow down and reflect on how all of these experiences are being woven into the fabric of their lives. How does what they learn in an economics class influence how they view issues of poverty and social injustice? Their classroom experience is about more than just getting an "A." It is about weaving together their experiences so they can shape a worldview that allows them to emerge as thoughtful Christian adults. As parents, what more could we ask than for our daughter or son to be able to address complex human problems by integrating biblical truth with their day-to-day experiences? This is a key component of the Christian college experience, and by asking good questions and providing the fertile soil for your daughter or son to reflect, you as a parent can play an important role in the process.

Conclusion

How has this happened? It seems just like yesterday you were helping your daughter take those first baby steps. Now she is ready to graduate and take those initial adult steps into life after college. When she was a baby, she clung tightly to your hand and tentatively put that first foot forward. Now she is ready to let go and walk confidently into the future. Unlike the characters in *St. Elmo's Fire*, your daughter has received a well-ordered Christian education that builds upon the strong foundation you provided. This foundation helped her cultivate God-given talents and a passionate commitment to pursue God's calling for her life. She has changed and matured into a thoughtful Christian adult, ready to face real-world problems and issues. Your role has changed as well. You have gone from being the director of her life to being a supporting actor. As parents, our responsibility to help our children listen to God's call is one that never ends. It simply changes in the way we serve as supporting agents in the divinely inspired process we call life.

CONCLUSION

O ur congregation recently had an abnormally large number of the youth group leave for college. While talking with some of the parents, I heard repeated comments like, "I knew this change would be hard, but I didn't know it would be this hard." My encouragement to these parents was simply to assure them that the pain they were feeling was natural and a sign of their love for their children. If their relationship with their daughters and sons was close, it was completely understandable that this transition would be deeply emotional. I also tried to help them understand that their daughters and sons still need them, though in new and different ways than before. This transition was as much a beginning as an end.

I hope that this book has shown you some of the ways your child still needs you. Her or his Christian college experience will come with challenges. However, if effective partnerships are forged among students, faculty members and administrators, and parents, a rich and rewarding experience awaits us all. A deep and abiding satisfaction comes when we discover the particular ways we have been called to offer praise and glory to our Creator. Please allow me to close by offering three suggestions which may also help you navigate this relationship you now share with your daughter or son.

First, please commit to pray steadfastly for your child. The decision to go away to a Christian college is an act of faith. Pray for the transition to college life. Pray for the cultivation of good study habits. Pray for wise social choices, including choices of friends and people to date. Pray that your child will find a church home that welcomes her or him. Please also pray that the Lord will grant us (the professors and administrators) wisdom, as we surely need the grace of God to effectively serve your child. Commit your child and the members of her or his institution to prayer during your own devotional time but also ask your church body to pray. Ask your fellow believers to pray for particular challenges your child may be facing. Nothing is more powerful than a great cloud of witnesses talking to God on behalf of our loved ones.

Second, remain committed to being a student of the institution where your daughter or son has enrolled. Informed parents are parents in the position to challenge the Christian college to fulfill its mission. Don't let us off easy and just read what we send you. Please take the time to read through additional materials such as the student handbook, the academic catalog, and the annual report. Read through the materials on the school's Web page and even the biographical information concerning your daughter or son's professors.

Third, remain in consistent communication with your child and ask specific questions about her or his experience. Ask about particular courses and particular professors. Ask about her or his thoughts concerning a major and how this choice fits into God's larger calling. Ask about the activities in which she or he is involved. Ask about new college friends and especially about anyone she or he might date. Demonstrate an abiding interest in your child's experience as well as the place she or he now calls home. In the end, the quality of these conversations is far more important than the quantity. You will get better information and be of better service to your child if you are poised to ask well-informed questions.

Finally, know when to insert yourself directly into your child's college experience should a serious problem arise. Ideally, you will never have to do this. But chances are that something will happen along the way where you may need to make a phone call or perhaps even come to campus beyond move-in day, parent's weekend, and the end of the academic year. If you are an informed parent, you will be able to recognize the difference between when your assistance would be productive and when it might prove counterproductive.

The Christian college experience can prove to be truly transformative for your daughter or son. I find it a great privilege each fall to receive the children of people who have poured so much into their lives. The Christian college can prove to be a place where all young people discover the unique ways they have been called to offer their lives in praise and worship of God. In life, all other questions will then prove secondary. Blessings.

For Additional Reading

For Parents Concerning the Christian College:

Benne, Robert. *Quality with Soul: How Six Premier Colleges and Universities Keep Faith with Their Religious Traditions.* Grand Rapids, Mich.: Eerdmans, 2001.

Dockery, David S. *Renewing Minds: Serving Church and Society through Christian Higher Education.* Nashville, Tenn.: B&H Academic, 2008.

Litfin, Duane. *Conceiving the Christian College.* Grand Rapids, Mich.: Eerdmans, 2004.

Marsden, George A. *The Soul of the American University: From Protestant Establishment to Established Nonbelief.* New York: Oxford University Press, 1996.

Noll, Mark A. *The Scandal of the Evangelical Mind.* Grand Rapids, Mich.: Eerdmans, 1995.

Ringenberg, William C. *The Christian College: A History of Protestant Higher Education in America.* Grand Rapids, Mich.: Baker Academic, 2006.

Smith, James K.A. *Desiring the Kingdom: Worship, Worldview, and Cultural Formation.* Grand Rapids, Mich.: Baker Academic, 2009.

To Recommend to Students:

Budziszewski, J. *How to Stay Christian in College.* Colorado, Springs, Colo.: NavPress, 2004.

Cosgrove, Mark P. *Foundations of Christian Thought: Faith, Learning, and the Christian Worldview.* Grand Rapids, Mich.: Kregel, 2006.

Holmes, Arthur F. *The Idea of a Christian College.* Grand Rapids, Mich.: Eerdmans, 1987.

Melleby, Derek. *Make College Count: A Faithful Guide to Life and Learning.* Grand Rapids, Mich.: Baker Books, 2011.

Opitz, Don, and Derek Melleby. *The Outrageous Idea of Academic Faithfulness: A Guide for Students.* Grand Rapids, Mich.: Brazos Press, 2007.

Ostrander, Rick. *Why College Matters to God: Faithful Learning and Christian Higher Education.* Abilene, Tex.: Abilene Christian University Press, 2009.

Plantinga, Cornelius. *Engaging God's World: A Christian Vision of Faith, Learning, and Living.* Grand Rapids, Mich.: Eerdmans, 2002.

ENDNOTES

FOREWORD

1. Stanley Fish, "Why We Built the Ivory Tower," *New York Times*, May 21, 2004; retrieved at http://query.nytimes.com/gst/fullpage.html?res=9E02E2DD113FF932A15756C0A9629C8B63&pagewanted=2.

2. Arthur F. Holmes, *Building the Christian Academy* (Grand Rapids, Mich.: Eerdmans, 2001).

3. Stanton L. Jones, "An Integration View," in E. Johnson, ed., *Psychology and Christianity: Five Views*, 2nd ed. (Downers Grove, Ill.: InterVarsity Press, 2010), 101-128.

INTRODUCTION

1 Bridget Booher, "Helicopter Parents," *Duke Magazine* (January-February 2007).

2 Betsa Marsh, "Helicopter Parents Hover over Campus," *Miamian Magazine* (Spring 2007).

3 Sara Lipka, "Helicopter Parents Help Students, Survey Finds," *The Chronicle of Higher Education* (November 2007).

CHAPTER 1

1 Augustine, *The Confessions*, trans. R. S. Pine-Coffin (New York, N.Y.: Penguin Classics), 21.

2 Parker Palmer, *Let Your Life Speak: Listening for the Voice of Vocation* (San Francisco: Jossey-Bass, 1999), 25.

3 "Statutes of Harvard, 1646," in *The History of Higher Education*, eds. Lester F. Goodchild and Harold S. Wechsler, 2nd ed. (Boston: Simon & Schuster, 1997), 125.

4 Alexander M. Astin, "Is Spirituality a Legitimate Concern in Higher Education?" (opening keynote address presented at

Spirituality and Learning Conference, San Francisco, April 18, 2002), 2-3.

5   Alan Wolfe, "A Welcome Revival of Religion in the Academy," *Chronicle of Higher Education* 44 (1997): B4-5.

6   Alexander M. Astin, Helen Astin, and Jennifer Lindholm, *Cultivating the Spirit: How Colleges Can Enhance Students' Inner Lives* (San Francisco: Jossey-Bass, 2011), 9.

7   Patrick Love and Donna Talbot, "Defining Spiritual Development: A Missing Consideration for Student Affairs," *NASPA Journal* 37.1 (1999): 364.

8   Ibid., 364-367.

9   Conrad Cherry, Betty De Berg, and Amanda Porterfield, "Religion on Campus," *Liberal Education,* 87.4 (2001): 6-14, and Patrick Love, "Spirituality and Student Development: Theoretical Connections," in Margaret Jablonski, ed., *The Implications of Student Spirituality for Student Affairs Practice* (San Francisco: Jossey-Bass, 2001), 7-16.

10 Alyssa N. Bryant, Jeung Yun Choi, and Maiko Yasuno, "Understanding the Religious and Spiritual Dimensions of Students' Lives in the First Year of College," *Journal of College Student Development* 44.6 (2003): 736.

11 Alexander W. Astin, et al., *The Spiritual Life of College Students: A National Study of College Students' Search for Meaning and Purpose* (Executive Summary) (Los Angeles: Higher Education Research Institute at UCLA, 2004), 4.

12 Jean Twenge, *Generation Me: Why Today's Young Americans Are More Confident, Assertive, Entitled—and More Miserable than Ever Before* (New York: Free Press, 2006), 35.

13 Arthur Chickering and Linda Reisser, *Education and Identity*, 2nd ed. (San Francisco: Jossey-Bass, 1993).

14 The preceding conversation about identity comes from James Marcia, "Development and Validation of Ego Identity Status," *Journal of Personality and Social Psychology* 3.5 (1966): 551-558.

15 Steve Beers, "Faith Development on the Christian College Campus," *Growth: Journal of the Association for Christians in Student Development* 3 (2003): 31-33.

16 William C. Ringenberg, *The Christian College: A History of Protestant Higher Education in America* (Grand Rapids, Mich.: Baker Academic, 2006).

17 William Straus and Neil Howe, *Millennials Go to College: Strategies for a New Generation on Campus* (Washington, DC: American Association of Collegiate Registrars, 2003).

18 Thomas L. Friedman, "Generation Q," *New York Times*, 10 October 2007, A23.

19 John David Brooks, "The Organizational Kid," *Atlantic Monthly* 287 (April 2001): 40-54.

20 Scott Seider and Howard Gardner, "The Fragmented Generation," *Journal of College & Character* 10.4 (April 2009): 1.

21 Ibid, 2.

22 Ibid.

23 David Kinnamon and Gabe Lyon, *UnChristian: What a New Generation Really Thinks about Christianity and Why It Really Matters* (Grand Rapids, Mich.: Baker Books, 2007).

24 Ibid., 23.

CHAPTER TWO

1 Neil Postman, *The End of Education: Redefining the Value of School* (New York: Vintage Books, 1995).

2 Ernest Pascarella, "Colleges Influence on Principled Moral Reasoning," *Educational Record*, 78.3 & 78.4 (Summer/Fall 1997).

3   Arthur F. Holmes, *All Truth Is God's Truth* (Downers Grove, Ill.: InterVarsity Press, 1983).

4   Lion Gardiner, *Redesigning Higher Education: Producing Dramatic Gains in Student Learning* (ASHE-ERIC Higher Education Reports Volume 23, No. 7), iii.

5   Alexander Astin, *What Matters in College? Four Critical Years Revisited* (San Francisco: Jossey-Bass, 1993).

6   Alexander Astin, "Student Involvement: A Developmental Theory for Higher Education," *Journal of College Student Development* 40.5 (September/October 1999).

7   Gardiner, *Redesigning,* 23-24.

8   Available on Youtube at: http://www.youtube.com/watch?v=kO8x8eoU3L4.

9   Gardiner, *Redesigning,* 46.

10 Ernest Pascarella and Patrick Terenzini, *How College Affects Students: A Third Decade of Research* (San Francisco: Jossey-Bass, 2005), 572-573.

11 Ibid., 574.

12 National Commission on Accountability in Higher Education, "Accountability for Better Results: A National Imperative for Higher Education," 2005 State Higher Education Executive Officers, 34.

13 Pascarella and Terenzini, *How College Affects Students.*

14 Baum, S. & Payea, K. "The Benefits of Higher Education for Individuals and Society," College Board: Education Pays 2004: Trends in Higher Education Series (2005).

15 "Are Big Name Universities Worth the Money?" *Newsweek,* Kaplan College Guide (2009).

16 "The Difference between a College Graduate and a High School Graduate Is $1 Million," U. S. College Search (2008).

17 "Are Big Name Universities Worth the Money?"

18 Holmes, *The Idea of the Christian College*, rev. ed. (Grand Rapids, Mich.: Eerdmans, 1987).

CHAPTER 3

1 National Survey of Student Engagement, *Assessment for Improvement: Tracking Student Engagement Over Time: Annual Results 2009* (Bloomington, Ind.: Indiana University Center for Postsecondary Research, 2009), 34.

2 "A Snapshot of Annual High-Risk College Drinking Consequences," NIAAA Task Force on College Drinking, National Institute on Alcohol Abuse and Alcoholism (NIAAA), http://www.collegedrinkingprevention.gov/ StatsSummaries/snapshot.aspx (accessed June 1, 2010).

3 George Kuh, "The Other Curriculum: Out-of-Class Experiences Associated with Student Learning and Personal Development," *Journal of Higher Education* 66.2 (1995): 123-155.

4 Neil Postman, *The End of Education: Redefining the Value of School* (New York: Vintage, 1996), 3-4.

5 Kuh, "The Other Curriculum."

6 Ibid., 145.

7 Ernest Pascarella and Patrick Terenzini, *How College Affects Students: A Third Decade of Research* (San Francisco: Jossey-Bass, 2005), 603.

8 Ibid.

9 Ana Arboleda, Yongyi Wang, Mack Shelly, and Donald Whalen, "Predictors of Residence Hall Involvement," *Journal of College Student Development* 44.4 (2003): 529.

10 Kuh, "The Other Curriculum," 123-155.

11 Christine Cress, Helen Astin, Kathleen Zimmerman-Oster, and John Burkhardt, "Developmental Outcomes of College Students' Involvement in Leadership Activities," *Journal of College Student Development* 42.1 (2001): 15-27.

12 Steven Bialek and Ann Groves Lloyd, "Post Graduation Impact of Student Leadership," American College Personnel Association Research Report: ERIC 1997: http://www.eric. ed.gov/PDFS/ED417669.pdf.

13 Robert Bringle and Judy Hatcher, "Implementing Service Learning in Higher Education," *Journal of Higher Education* 67.2 (1996): 222.

14 Ibid., 221-238.

15 Gregory Markus, Jeffrey Howard, and David King, "Integrating Community Service and Classroom Instruction Enhances Learning: Results from an Experiment," *Educational Evaluation and Policy Analysis* 15.4 (1993): 410-419.

16 Pascarella and Terenzini, *How College Affects Students.*

17 Kuh, et al. "Student Learning Imperative," American College Personnel Association (1996).

18 William H. Willimon and Thomas H. Naylor, *Abandoned Generation: Rethinking Higher Education* (Grand Rapids, Mich.: Eerdmans, 1995)

CHAPTER 4

1 Kim S. Phipps, "Epilogue: Campus Climate and Christian Scholarship," *Scholarship and Christian Faith: Enlarging the Conversation,* eds. Douglas Jacobsen and Rhonda Hustedt Jacobsen (New York: Oxford University Press, 2004), 171.

2 Alexander Astin, *What Matters in College: Four Critical Years Revisited* (San Francisco: Jossey-Bass, 1993), 398.

3   Nancy Evans, Deanna Forney, and Florence Guido-DiBrito, *Student Development in College: Theory, Research, and Practice* (San Francisco: Jossey-Bass, 1998), 111.

4   Ibid, 112.

5   Richard Kadison and Theresa Foy DiGeronimo, *College of the Overwhelmed: The Campus Mental Health Crisis and What to Do about It* (San Francisco: Jossey-Bass, 2004), 5.

6   Ibid., 240.

7   Barry Guinagh, "Homesickness in the Freshman Year," *Journal of the Freshman Year Experience* 4.1 (1992): 111-120.

8   Maria Urani, Steven Miller, James Johnson, and Thomas Petzel, "Homesickness in Socially Anxious First-Year College Students," *College Student Journal* 37.3 (2003): 392-399.

9   Ibid., 395.

10 Walter Buboltz, Franklin Brown, and Barlow Soper, "Sleep Habits and Patterns of College Students: A Preliminary Study," *Journal of American College Health* 50.3 (2001): 131-135.

11 Ibid., 564.

12 Two seminal sources for information on the critical nature of the first-year college experience are Alexander Astin's, *What Matters in College: Four Critical Years Revisited* (San Francisco, CA: Jossey Bass, 1997); and *Challenging and Supporting the First-Year Student: A Handbook for Improving the First Year of College*, eds. Lee Upcraft, John Gardner, and Betsy Barefoot (San Francisco: Jossey-Bass, 2004).

13 Rueben Welch, *We Really Do Need Each Other* (Nashville, Tenn.: Impact Books, 1973).

14 William Strauss and Neil Howe, *Millenials Go to College: Strategies for a New Generation on Campus* (Washington, DC: American Association of College Registrars, 2003).

15 For detailed information regarding the Family Educational Right to Privacy Act, refer to the Department of Education Web site at ED.gov.

CHAPTER 5

1 Nancy Evans, Deanna Forney, and Florence Guido-DiBrito, *Student Development in College: Theory, Research, and Practice* (San Francisco: Jossey-Bass, 1998), 7.

2 Tammy L. Lewis and Richard A. Niesenbaum, "The Benefits of Short-Term Study Abroad," *Chronicle of Higher Education, Review* 51 (2005): B20.

3 James Posey, "Study Abroad: Education and Employment Outcomes of Participants versus Non-Participants." Doctoral dissertation, Department of Education Leadership and Policy Studies (Florida State University, 2003), 11.

4 Mary Dwyer and Courtney Peters, "The Benefits of Study Abroad," *Transitions Abroad Magazine* (March/April 2004): 1.

5 Ibid.

6 Robert Priest, Terry Dischinger, Steve Rasmussen, and C. M. Brown, "Researching the Short-Term Mission Movement," *Missiology* 34.4 (2006): 431-450.

7 Kurt Ver Beek, "The Impact of Short-Term Missions: A Case Study of House Construction in Honduras after Hurricane Mitch," *Missiology* 34.4 (2006): 477-495.

8 David Johhnstone, "Closing the Loop: Debriefing and the Short-Term College Missions Team," *Missiology* 34.4 (2006): 528.

9 Andrew Furco, "Service-Learning: A Balanced Approach to Experiential Education," *Expanding Boundaries: Service and Learning* (1996): 5.

10 Alexander Astin, Lori Vogelgesang, Elaine Ikeda, and Jennifer Yee, *How Service-Learning Affects Students,* Unpublished

manuscript, Higher Education Research Institute (Los Angeles: University of California, 2000).

11 Ernest Pascarella and Patrick Terenzini, *How College Affects Students* (San Francisco: Jossey-Bass, 2005).

12 Karen Leppel, "The Impact of Major on College Persistence among Freshmen," *Higher Education* 41.3 (2001): 327-342.

13 Myers Brigs, 1998-2010, HumanMetrics.

14 The Strengths Finder was developed by Clifton and is copyrighted by the Gallup Organization, 2007. To learn more about this assessment instrument, see Tom Rath, *Now Discover Your Strengths* (Gallup Press, 2007).

15 Career Direct Complete Guidance System (Crown Financial Ministries, 2010).

16 Campbell Skills and Strengths Inventory (CSSI) (Pearson Education, Inc., 2009).

17 Arthur Holmes, *The Idea of the Christian College*, rev. ed. (Grand Rapids, Mich.: Eerdmans, 1987).

CHAPTER 6

1 Cornelius Plantinga, Jr., *Engaging God's World: A Christian Vision of Faith, Loving, and Learning* (Grand Rapids, Mich.: Eerdmans, 2002), 33.

2 Ibid., 94.

3 Sara Lipka, "In Campus-Crime Reports, There's Little Safety in the Numbers," http://chronicle.com/article/In-Campus-Crime-Reports-Th/30058/ (accessed January 7, 2011).

4 U.S. Department of Education, "Summary Campus Crime Data, 2006-2008: Disciplinary Actions," http://ed.gov/admins/lead/safety/arrests2006-08.pdf (accessed June 2, 2010), 1,4,6.

5 Arthur Chickering and Linda Reisser, *Education and Identity* (San Francisco: Jossey-Bass, 1993).

6   Nancy Shute, "Mental Health Problems Common on College Campuses," *U. S. News & World Report*, http://health.usnews. com/usnews/health/articles/070417/17vatech.mentalhealth. htm (accessed January 7, 2011).

7   Higher Education Research Institute (HERI), *2009 CIRP Freshman Survey* (Los Angeles: UCLA Press, 2009).

8   Ibid.

9   Richard Kadison and Theresa Foy DiGeronimo, *College of the Overwhelmed: The Campus Mental Health Crisis and What to Do about It* (San Francisco: Jossey-Bass, 2004).

10   Ibid., 5.

11   David Downey, "Depression's Influence on Involvement," (M. A. Thesis, Taylor University, 2010).

12   Ibid.

13   Bonnie S. Fisher, Francis T. Cullen, and Michael G. Turner, *The Sexual Victimization of College Women* (Washington, DC: United States Department of Justice, 2000), 10.

14   Report of the National Postsecondary Education Cooperative: Information Required to be Disclosed under the Higher Education Act of 1965 (National Postsecondary Education Cooperative, November 2009), http://nces.ed.gov, (accessed January 14, 2011).

15   Health Insurance Portability and Accountability Act, 1996.

CHAPTER 7

1   Susan M. Farmer and Edward E. Brown, "College Students and the Work World," *Journal of Employment Counseling* 45.3 (2008): 108.

2   D. G. Kennedy, "Eureka!," *American Demographics* (June 1, 2004). http://findarticles.com/p/articles/mi_m4021/is_5_26/ ai_n6077841 (accessed May 15, 2010).

3   Farmer and Brown, "College Students and the Work World," 109.

4   Christian Smith and Patricia Snell, *Souls in Transition: The Religious & Spiritual Lives of Emerging Adults* (New York: Oxford University Press, 2009), 6.

5   John N. Gardner, "The Senior Year Experience," *About Campus* 4.1 (1999): 6.

6   Ibid, 7.

7   Arthur W. Chickering and Linda Reisser, *Education and Identity*, 2nd edition (San Francisco: Jossey-Bass, 1993).

8   Farmer and Brown, "College Students and Work World," 111.

9   William C. Spohn, "The Chosen Path," *America* 189.2 (2003): 11.

10 The Project on Student Debt: An Initiative on the Institute for Access & Success. Quick Facts About College Debt. http://projectonstudentdebt.org/files/File/Debt_Facts_and_Sources.pdf (accessed July 14, 2010).

11 Ellen Bradburn, Rachael Berger, Xiaojie Li, Katharin Peter, and Kathryn Rooney, "Baccalaureate and Beyond: A Descriptive Summary of 1999-2000 Bachelor's Degree Recipients, 1 Year Later—With an Analysis of Time to Degree" (2003). http://nces.ed.gov/pubsearch/pubsinfo.asp?pubid=2003165 (accessed May 27, 2010).

12 Smith and Snell, *Souls in Transition*.

INDEX

About the Authors

Todd C. Ream (Ph.D., Penn State) is the senior scholar for faith and scholarship and associate professor of humanities with the John Wesley Honors College at Indiana Wesleyan University. He has served in a number of roles in student development. His previous books include *Christian Faith and Scholarship* and *Christianity and Moral Identity in Higher Education* (both with Perry L. Glanzer). He also serves as the book review editor (with Perry L. Glanzer) for *Christian Scholar's Review* and *Christian Higher Education*. Todd and his family live in Greentown, Indiana, where they are members of Jerome Christian Church.

Timothy W. Herrmann (Ph.D., Indiana State) is professor of Higher Education and the chair of the Master of Arts in Higher Education program at Taylor University. He has served in a number of roles in student development and is a former president of the Association for Christians in Student Development (ACSD). He serves as the co-editor (with C. Skip Trudeau) for *Growth: The Journal of the Association for Christians in Student Development*. Tim and his family live in Upland, Indiana, where they are members of Upland Community Church.

C. Skip Trudeau (Ed.D., Indiana) is the dean of student development at Taylor University. He has served in a number of roles in student development and is a former president of the Association for Christians in Student Development (ACSD). He serves as the co-editor (with Timothy W. Herrmann) for *Growth: The Journal of the Association for Christians in Student Development*. Skip and his family live in Upland, Indiana, where they are members of Upland Community Church.